Eddie Van
Biogra[
The Life and Legacy of the
Guitar Star

CW00493639

Copyright © 2023 by Eric R Knull
All rights reserved.

The content of this book may not be reproduced, duplicated, or transmitted without the author's or publisher's express written permission. Under no circumstances will the publisher or author be held liable or legally responsible for any damages, reparation, or monetary loss caused by the information contained in this book, whether directly or indirectly.

Legal Notice:
This publication is copyrighted. It is strictly for personal use only. You may not change, distribute, sell, use, quote, or paraphrase any part of this book without the author's or publisher's permission.

Disclaimer Notice:
Please keep in mind that the information in this document is only for educational and entertainment purposes. Every effort has been made to present accurate, up-to-date, reliable, and comprehensive information. There are no express or implied warranties. Readers understand that the author is not providing legal, financial, medical, or professional advice. This book's content was compiled from a variety of sources. Please seek the advice of a licensed professional before attempting any of the techniques described in this book. By reading this document, the reader agrees that the author is not liable for any direct or indirect losses incurred as a result of using the information contained within this document, including, but not limited to, errors, omissions, or inaccuracies.

CONTENTS

Chapter 1: Small Dreamer

Jan van Halen, his wife Eugenia, and their two sons, Edward, age seven, and Alex, age eight, left their apartment at Rozemarijnstraat 59 in Nijmegen in the hazy half-light of the early morning of March 1, 1962. They were headed for the port of Rotterdam, a Tourist Class cabin on the SS Ryndam, and ultimately, the faraway shores of America.

The family had an upright Rippen piano, 75 Dutch guilders, and three huge luggage with them. Jan van Halen, a clarinetist and saxophonist who has been playing professionally since he was in his late teens, had spent much of his adult life traveling. He had boarded planes, trains, and cars to perform in a string of well-known jazz ensembles, swing bands, and orchestras. He believed that by embarking on this journey into the unknown, he would finally be able to seize possibilities that would let him play the conductor.

The forty-two-year-old musician donned his sharpest suit every evening of the first week of March 1962 to perform popular standards and ragtime and swing compositions above the soft burr of conversational babble and the delicate clinking of silvered cutlery on fine bone china in the ship's First Class restaurant. This was done to help pay for his family's transatlantic journey. The van Halen kids had a chance to perform on the family piano one evening, and they delighted their audience with a recital of meticulously performed, melodic European waltzes. The captain of the ship was so enchanted by the family that he invited them to sit at his table for dinner the next night. Edward van Halen, a small boy, took in the splendor of his new surroundings, tugged at his father's sleeve, and asked one straightforward inquiry while servers flitted attentively around the SS Ryndam's newest VIP guests:
Can't we just settle down here?

***

When thinking on his family's immigration experience, Eddie Van Halen said in 2015, "I have to hand it to my dad for having the balls, at the age of 42, to sell everything, pack his bags and come to a whole new country." The choice to move her small children from Holland to America at the beginning of the 1960s was actually made by Eugenia van Halen. Despite her husband's charm and assurance, people closest to the family understood that Eugenia always made the important decisions. This was something that Jan's friends and his naughty sons were never reluctant to point out to him.

In Holland, starting over offered additional difficulties. Since professional jazz musician engagements were becoming increasingly rare as the 'Big Band' era came to an end, Jan frequently had to take extended trips away from the marital residence for weeks or even months at a period in order to pursue new career chances. In fact, he was traveling when Eugenia gave birth to the couple's baby, whom they named Alexander Arthur van Halen, on May 8, 1953. Jan would also be missing when the family welcomed a second son, Edward Lodewijk, on January 26, 1955. Eugenia would frequently point this out to her husband during their frequent heated arguments in the family home. After the birth of her second child, Eugenia became increasingly frustrated with Jan's lack of support and insisted that the family move from Amsterdam to Nijmegen, the oldest city in the Netherlands, in the province of Gelderland, where Jan had relatives eager to help with the parenting responsibilities he so blithely neglected.

Edward and Alex were best friends since birth, or, as the younger of the two boys liked to say, "two peas in a pod." Their earliest years would have a soundtrack composed of Jan's songs. When heavy black shellac 78s were put on the family stereo and the house shook to the martial beats of up-tempo military marches, the usually boisterous pair would sit becalmed, enraptured, and fascinated while their father practiced his clarinet. They would also gleefully stomp around their living room, bashing and thrashing pots and pans. The boys would be taken to Jan's gigs when Eugenia was required to work night shifts in one of the part-time service industry jobs she had taken on because she had been denied white-collar employment opportunities by companies that openly discriminated against women of color. Their mother did this in the hopes that their presence would lessen her husband's propensity for lengthy post-gig drinking marathons. Instead, much to Eugenia's growing annoyance, it served only to strengthen the bond between the three of them, with Alex and Edward enjoying being transported to a different reality and returning from each outing more and more fascinated by their father's high-spirited, bohemian friends and their carefree, laissez-faire attitude toward rules, regulations, and responsibilities.

Eugenia was quick to see and unwillingly accept that her sons had their father's real curiosity and enthusiasm for music, despite the fact that she never concealed her dislike for her husband's wandering way of life. So, when Alex was six years old and Edward was five, she enrolled her kids in piano lessons with a local Russian concert pianist.

***

The Van Halen brothers faced their own teething issues. When Alex and Eddie first arrived in the US, they could only speak four words of English: "yes," "no," "motorcycle," and, somewhat haphazardly, "accident." Their education in the customs of their new environment was quick and frequently brutal; their first days at Alexander Hamilton Elementary School on Rose Villa Street were marked by racist threats, bullying, and irrational acts of violence.

Eddie remembered, "It was beyond terrible, it was absolutely terrifying. We attended a segregated school at the time, and because we didn't speak the language, we were viewed as a minority. Black people were my first pals in America. The white people were bullies; they had me eat playground sand and tore up my homework assignments. The black youngsters defended me.

One afternoon, Alex was out for a stroll in the neighborhood park when an older white boy with a Louisville Slugger passed by. Alex pointed at the bat and yelled, "Baseball!" eager to display a new word he had recently added to his limited vocabulary. The little child was stopped and asked a question by the teenager that he couldn't understand, to which the impudent but always courteous Dutch lad replied with a smile and a nod of the head. A few seconds later, while his attacker was walking away smiling, the victim fell on his knees in horror while holding a bloody, broken nose. The inquiry was, "Do you want me to hit you in the face with this?" it turned out.

Naturally, such terrifying occurrences bonded the Van Halen guys closer than two coats of creosote.

Eddie remarked, "We were two outsiders who didn't know the language and what was going on. "So, we learned to stick together and became best friends."

Music offered some continuity with calmer and more tranquil times amid the turmoil of this transitional period. Jan started playing gigs in wedding bands and oompah groups with musicians she met in local taverns to supplement the family's meager income, and Alex and Eddie were re-enrolled in piano lessons by their mother as soon as money allowed. Stasys 'Stanley' Kalvaitis, a fellow immigrant from Lithuania who graduated from St. Petersburg's prestigious Imperial Conservatory with violin prodigy Jascha Heifetz and world-renowned Ukrainian composer Sergei Prokofiev, served as their older teacher. Eddie disliked the accomplished Kalvaitis' strict, demanding teaching style and found his rote-learning lessons to be boring. He pretended to be attentive while choosing to play difficult recitals by ear instead of learning to read sheet music, engaging in his own quiet, low-key form of disobedience. Even if the Lithuanian maestro had been tricked, he was still a good judge of his student's talent because, in August 1964, when he entered Eddie in the third Southwestern Youth Music Festival at Long Beach City College, he urged Eugenia and Jan to go see their son represent the family with honor. Eddie didn't let his parents down and dutifully won first place in his category, but he didn't seem to care about the honor quite as much as they did.

The British music scene was of limited appeal to American consumers at the beginning of the 1960s because it was bland, conservative, and painfully well-mannered. Vera Lynn, the "Forces Sweetheart," was the only British musician to have a US number 1 single in the 1950s; otherwise, clean-cut British rock 'n' rollers like Cliff Richard, Adam Faith, and Billy Fury were mocked for being pale, flaccid, and completely irrelevant copies of their Sun Records counterparts. While the Tornados, Fury's backup band, achieved the first Billboard Hot 100 chart-topper by a British group in December 1962 with their instrumental, "Telstar," British artists mainly remained unheard of in the US throughout the Van Halen family's first year of residence in California.

That would change with the Beatles. Even though the band did not immediately find success in the US (their first two UK number 1 singles, "Please Please Me" and "From Me to You"), the release of the exhilaratingly bubbly "I Want to Hold Your Hand" sent a spike of adrenaline straight to the center of the US music business. Demand for their 45 exceeded supply even before their historic appearance on The Ed Sullivan Show on CBS television on February 9, 1964, which was seen by an estimated 73 million people. As a result, their record label, Capitol, was forced to outsource some of the pressing and production of the seven-inch vinyl disc to rival companies Columbia and RCA in order to meet the unprecedented demand. The song, the first of seven number-one singles the Liverpool band would record in that year, peaked at the top of the Billboard Hot 100 chart on February 1 and remained there for seven weeks. The Beatles' first album for Capitol, Meet the Beatles!, sold 3.6 million copies by the end of March, making it the best-selling record in history up to that date. A number of UK chart singles were repackaged and quickly released for the American market as a result of the Liverpool group's extraordinary success, which inspired both US record labels and fans to take a fresh look at the previously dormant UK music scene.

Oddly enough, despite the Beatles' dominance of the airways, it was their more polite counterparts, the Dave Clark Five, who introduced Eddie Van Halen to rock 'n' roll. The Londoners' "Glad All Over," which had dethroned "I Want to Hold Your Hand" from the top of the British singles chart earlier in the year, entered the Billboard Top 10 in April 1964, the same historic week in which the Beatles secured the top five spots on the Hot 100. Its popularity sparked the first rumors of a probable "British Invasion" of the US pop charts, and one young immigrant boy's life was forever changed by its heavily accented whomp in the summer of 1964.

The Van Halen boys made the decision to start their first band that summer. Eddie played the piano, Alex played the saxophone, Kevan Hill, a fellow Hamilton Elementary School student, played the guitar.

Brian Hill, Kevan's brother, played the drums, and Don Ferris, a neighbor, played the second saxophone for The Broken Combs. The quintet composed two original songs, "Rumpus" and the intriguingly titled "Boogie Booger," and performed them at the school's dining hall alongside renditions of British Invasion standards. The boys' transformation from mistrusted outsiders to schoolyard heroes happened very immediately, and it did wonders for their self-esteem and social abilities, even if they still had a healthy skepticism of their old tormentors.

Jan offered to replace Eddie's flimsy cardboard drum kits with something more substantial, delighted by his sons' growing interest in the process of creating their own music. Eddie accepted, and Jan duly bought him a $125 Japanese-made St George kit, which he promised to pay for with the money from his morning newspaper delivery round. After agreeing to this arrangement, the youngster was more than a little miffed to discover that his labor of love was being taken advantage of by his older brother, who could be found pounding on the kit each morning as Eddie returned from his early-morning deliveries while ignoring the flamenco guitar he had been given.

But Eddie was conscious that he needed a new tool if he wanted to accurately reproduce the stinging, aggressive, and reverb-drenched sound of California's surf-guitar legends. His first electric guitar was eventually acquired through a trip to the Sears department store. It was a $110 Japanese-made Teisco Del Rey model that Eddie recalled choosing solely because it had four pickups, one more than any other guitar in the store. Jan gave him his first amplifier, which Eddie modified with a Radio Shack converter. It was manufactured at home by a Pasadena neighbor.

The Van Halen boys would soon have an overwhelming array of options for "grunge noise." 1967 saw the release of Sgt. Pepper's Lonely Hearts Club Band, The Doors, The Velvet Underground, and Nico, The Piper at the Gates of Dawn by Pink Floyd, Their Satanic Majesties Request by the Rolling Stones, and Are You Experienced and Axis: Bold as Love by the Jimi Hendrix Experience. However, one album in particular captured the brothers' attention: Disraeli

Gears, the second release from British rock supergroup' Cream. It was a showcase for the prodigious talents of bassist Jack Bruce, drummer Ginger Baker, and former Yardbirds/Bluesbreakers member Eric Clapton, who was regarded as the most exciting young guitarist in the world at the age of twenty-two by peers, critics, and music fans alike.

Eddie thought Clapton's tone and phrasing sounded like a tenor sax, bringing to mind, at least subconsciously, warm, happy recollections of his father's playing in simpler times in Holland. Eddie also detected echoes of the late-night jazz sessions he and Alex had attended as kids in Cream's brave, unrestrained, virtuoso performance.

The group made music thrilling in a manner I don't believe people really understood,' he later told Guitar World.

It seemed almost as if the song's lyrics and musical structure were incidental. "Let's get this shit over with so we can make music and see where we land tonight."

At their new school, Jefferson Elementary on East Villa Street, the Van Halen brothers created their own "power trio" with Eddie's classmate Jim Wright on bass. They were inspired by the English group. The group, originally known as the Sounds of Las Vegas and eventually simply the Sounds, performed surf music, Beatles and Monkees favorites, and, of course, whatever Cream tunes they could learn.

Jan Van Halen took notice of the budding group's abilities and started "borrowing" Alex and then Eddie (as a bassist) for his own performances, playing "weddings, bar mitzvahs, polkas, and all that other shit," as Eddie recounted.

Eddie recalled the boys as "the little freak sideshow" who occasionally performed as their father's opening act or intermission entertainment. Naturally, the twelve-year-old youngster was first nervous about such commitments, which Jan attempted to relieve with his own tried-and-true, if unique, methods.

When I was 12 years old, my dad introduced me to drinking and smoking, Eddie recalled. He said, "Here," in response to my nervousness. Take a vodka shot. Boom, my anxiety vanished.

At the conclusion of one such night, as was customary, Jan Van Halen shared his fedora around the audience and requested that they provide something concrete to demonstrate their appreciation for the night's entertainment. The hat came back from its circuit with $22 in it. Jan gave his sidekicks Alex and Eddie $5 each after taking a portion of the proceeds. Although the boys were not yet aware of American labor rules, they were not so immature that they were blind to the unfairness of this revenue distribution, and they expressed their outrage at it. Their father merely provided a shrug and a smile.

Chapter 2: On Fire

Editor of Guitar Player magazine Don Menn flung open the door to his office and invited journalists Jas Obrecht and Tom Wheeler, as well as editor of Keyboard magazine Tom Darter, to join him in his sanctuary. The trio waited anxiously as Menn strolled across the room to his record player, carefully raised the tonearm, and dropped the stylus on the run-in groove introducing the second track on the red vinyl EP spinning on the turntable. They expected either a reprimand or a business update. As an over-distorted cascading flurry of quick-fire triads and screaming pinch harmonics filled the air, he asked his hushed colleagues, "What is that?" What is that, he asked again.

Although Ted Templeman had spent countless long hours carefully going over the 25-song demo recorded at Sunset Sound in April 1977 in order to compile the strongest song selection for Van Halen's debut album and isolate particular verses, bridges, and choruses from weaker cuts that could possibly be cleaved, grafted, or repurposed elsewhere during pre-production, 'Eruption' hadn't been identified as a potential cornerstone of the recording. Eddie Van Halen's technically brilliant guitar instrumental wasn't on the initial tape reel, so this wasn't a careless blunder. In fact, toward the end of the recording sessions, when producer Templeman stepped out of the control booth at Sunset Sound to get a coffee, he overheard the guitarist improvising variations on a classical theme. This was the first time the producer heard what would later become the album's signature musical motif.

Whoa, what's that? Templeman made a query.
Ah, nothing," Van Halen responded. Just something to get me warmed up.
Let's listen to it one more time, the producer said. We must capture it. Without delay.
Donn Landee was told to turn on the monitors by Templeman as he entered the control booth.
The engineer must be told, "We've got to record this," according to Templeman.

Landee reassured him, "Rolling already."

For the better part of three years, Eddie Van Halen had been honing his solo performance onstage in Hollywood bars. He would frequently play the dramatic instrumental with his back to the audience, making it impossible for anyone to see what he was playing. With ukulele-playing "Wizard of the Strings," the guitarist was hiding a secret method in which he used both of his hands on the fretboard to tap out notes at breakneck speed. Roy Smeck, Jimmie Webster, Dave Bunker, Barney Kessel, Steve Hackett of Genesis, and Harvey Mandel of Canned Heat, a musician Eddie admired, all deserved credit for their own pioneering contributions to expanding the vocabulary of the instrument in this way, but Van Halen's tumbling arpeggiated torrents elevated the technique into an art form.

Van Halen would explain it to Steven Rosen of Guitar World by saying, "It's like having a sixth finger on your left hand." You're striking a fretboard note rather than picking the guitar. No one was actually doing much more than a quick stretch and note. I therefore began playing around.

On the rumor mills of Hollywood, information spreads quickly. When local favorites Van Halen signed with Warner Bros., making them the first band of the new wave of young groups to work their way through the local clubs onto a major label, the echoes of Ted Templeman and Mo Ostin's footsteps had barely stopped echoing in the Starwood's hallways on February 11, 1977. The contracts were signed by Marshall Berle and Dr. Roth's assigned lawyer Dennis Bond, and the ink had just about dried when LA music scene hype guru Kim Fowley wrote the group's first print feature in Phonograph Record in May.

"On the general rock history and geographical relevance of Hollywood, one need not write any introduction," Fowley penned. Hollywood is Los Angeles, and since California is represented by Los Angeles, Hollywood is the big time! There is just one option this year for up-and-coming, deserving new talent: Van Halen!

A modern-day Black Oak Arkansas, Van Halen have recently signed with Warner Brothers Records and are only a few steps away from the level of rock glory established by Led Zeppelin during their "Squeeze My Lemon" heyday. Ed Van Halen, a genius on the lead guitar, will alter a lot of lives all around the world in the upcoming year, according to lead singer Dave Roth.
There is no pressure, therefore.

Ted Templeman couldn't reserve the space for Van Halen until late August of 1977 since he had already committed to using Sunset Sound during the spring and summer of that year to record the Doobie Brothers' seventh studio album. To his own astonishment, as the scheduled time became near, the producer's level of experience caused him to feel more anxious than his inexperienced protégés did. According to Templeman's own account, which was shared with his biographer Greg Renoff, he developed an "obsession" with perfecting every aspect of the California quartet's debut album. I was crazy, he thought. I aimed for perfection.

Despite the praise bestowed upon his work with Van Morrison, Little Feat, and Captain Beefheart, Templeman's failure to bring Californian hard-rockers Montrose mainstream commercial success nevertheless hurt on a personal and professional level. He saw in Van Halen not only another hard rock band from the Golden State with even more talent and reach, but also a chance for personal atonement. Templeman's doubts about Roth's vocal prowess actually led him to wonder what this powerhouse of a band might accomplish with a more 'traditional' singer front and center, such as, say, former Montrose frontman Sammy Hagar. He would only discuss these concerns with his dependable and discrete wingman Landee, though. The producer learned to appreciate Roth's distinctive phrasing, absurd tongue-in-cheek ad libs, and his irreverent, off-kilter perspectives on well-known lyrical motifs over the weeks between the group's blitzkrieg demo session in April and their return to Sunset Sound on August 29. He was also impressed that Roth decided to enroll in vocal lessons before returning to the studio, showing that he was willing to work hard for the greater good despite Bill Aucoin's scathing critiques still residing rent-free in his head.

Templeman explained to his staff his plans for the sessions after being hired by Sunset Sound. Gene Simmons promised that he and Landee would keep things simple and organic and strive to cut nearly every track live off the floor, without overdubs, in order to faithfully replicate the pure, bombastic energy of the band's live shows. He was aware that the quartet disliked Gene Simmons's fussy and meticulous working practices at Electric Lady.

Landee reasoned, "They'd barely had any studio experience." We really wanted to get them before they really realized what they were doing — just have them come in and play and then get them out. It was evident that over time they would become skilled at creating records, but at that moment, we really wanted to get them.

Eddie was delighted by the suggested minimalist approach because Simmons' meticulously layered multitracking in New York had taken much of the fun and spontaneity out of the recording process for the guitarist.
"Gene said, "Here's what you do in the studio - you play your rhythm sections on one track, and your solo parts on another,"" Eddie remembered. I can still clearly recall how awkward it felt to separate my rhythm sections from my lead and fill parts. I had grown accustomed to performing both concurrently on stage. I would simply daydream in between chords. I didn't think to ask, "Can't I play just like I play live?," since it was my first time in a recording studio.

Three instruments and three voices make up "Van Halen, with hardly any overdubs." I detest overdubbing because playing with the boys is just more fun. There isn't any emotion there to base your work on.
Templeman recalls that the group initially set up in Sunset Sound's Studio 2, although the studio's contemporaneous paperwork indicates that Studio 1 was really used first. Templeman and Landee then moved the group between the two rooms based on their availability. Although it is widely believed that the quartet completed the album in just twenty-one days, the original invoices for the sessions from Sunset Sound Recorders show that the group spent a total of thirty-three days at the location, working from midday to six o'clock each day.

Michael Anthony and the Van Halen siblings set up as if playing a club gig or jamming in Roth's basement, with Roth sequestered in the vocal booth but able to maintain eye contact with his bandmates at all times. Every day the tapes began to play after a few sneaky lines of "krell" (band jargon for cocaine) were hoovered away from the grownups' view. Simple. The session got underway with the tracking of "Atomic Punk" on August 30. The following day, tape was laid down for "Feel Your Love Tonight," "Runnin' with the Devil," "Ain't Talkin' 'Bout Love," and "You Really Got Me" by the Kinks. Templeman and Landee would choose their favorite take after two or three attempts at each song, send the Van Halen lads and Anthony home for the day, and then start the time-consuming process of coaxing a decent vocal take from Roth. Templeman later acknowledged, "It took forever, sometimes, to get Dave on point," but the Van Halen brothers didn't need to be aware of that at the time. The producer would listen back to preliminary desk mixes every night, completely certain that something remarkable was taking place.

People frequently enquire about how Templeman obtained such a remarkable sound from Ed, he added. "The solution is straightforward: I positioned the correct speaker and microphone, then took a step back. Ed is truly the only one responsible. Since I thought it was the most amazing thing I had ever heard, my strategy was to simply take the guitar and blow it up all over the face of the damn map.

Templeman remarked, "Donn Landee is such a great engineer, he really took a major part in capturing that raw guitar sound." But at the Starwood, Edward essentially had that sound of his.
Eddie concurred, saying, "What Ted was able to do was record our live sound."

According to him, Sunset Sound is simply a large space that is comparable to our basement, as he told Guitar World's Steven Rosen. It was a party, according to the guys who operated the studio and kept the place clean. 'There were beer cans all over the floor and Pink's hot dog smears all over the place,' they recalled when we were through. It was fantastic that we performed just as we did on stage. There was no sense that we were recording a record. We simply entered, drank a couple beers, and played.

This casual, subtle, and unassuming portrayal of the album recording sessions was very Eddie. A more comprehensive account of events can be found in Templeman's autobiography A Platinum Producer's Life in Music, in which he expresses his complete delight at the young man's attention to detail, openness to novel ideas, politeness, and absolutely amazing improvisational abilities. It was quite poignant to observe Eddie, despite his apparent brilliance, get anxious before takes and frequently ask Templeman for confirmation that he had performed as needed. The producer occasionally caught himself slipping into "awed fanboy" mode, feeling honored to be sharing the same creative space with the guitarist, whom he would later praise as one of the greatest performers in history.

Templeman told Rolling Stone, "I knew he was a guitar genius from the first rehearsal." Actually, I had never witnessed anything quite like that until I watched him perform at the Starwood. Charlie Parker, Art Tatum, and this youngster are the three jazz greats.Because I worked with guitarists in so many bands, like Montrose, the Doobie Brothers, and Van Morrison, I had a solid reference. He was pretty freaking good, Ronnie Montrose. Ed is totally above all that garbage, I thought when I saw him. This is something from another planet.

The album had been recorded, mixed, and mastered by the middle of October for a reasonable cost of between $46,000 and $54,000, depending on whose accounting abilities you trust. Whatever the case, Van Halen unquestionably sounded like a million bucks as the stylus landed on its grooves. Warners were over the moon, but when the band saw the album artwork that the label's creative director had planned to impose upon them, they were noticeably less delighted. The suggested cover image depicted the quartet as melancholy, sullen punks, a look that was quite popular in 1977 but hardly an appropriate portrayal of this band or their Big Rock sound. It was taken after sunset on the grounds of Dr. Roth's Pasadena estate.

Eddie remembered, "They tried to make us look like The Clash." We came up with the Van Halen logo and told them to put it on the record after saying, "Fuck this shit!" We were trying to say, "Hey, we're just a rock 'n' roll band, don't try and slot us with the Sex Pistols thing just because it's becoming popular."

To avoid making the same mistakes again, Warners' art director Dave Bhang hired German-born, Los Angeles-based photographer Elliot Gilbert for a reshoot and invited him to meet the band at the record label's Burbank office before the shoot to get a genuine sense of their personalities, aesthetic, and sound.

Gilbert remembers that "Ted Templeman was there, and the four guys in the band, and they gave me a cassette of the album." The guys remained silent, but David handed me a large jar of marijuana and commanded me to "Make me look like cock and balls." I was never really sure what that meant.

The new session happened during what the photographer refers to as "the rock 'n' roll hours," not at the Whisky a Go Go as has sometimes been falsely stated. Instead, it happened at Gilbert's photo studio on Curson Avenue in Los Angeles.

He recalls that everyone was smoking and having a fantastic time around three in the morning. They sort of put up a performance for me in my studio, and I would simply bring people in at random and ask them to pose for my camera. Eddie calmly smoked his cigarette and smiled while David was bouncing in and out of the picture. They appeared cool, like a group with something interesting to say.

After one pre-release crisis was resolved, another drama suddenly appeared on the horizon. Moreover, this time the loose-lipped Dutch guitarist was directly to fault. After the album sessions were finished, Eddie and Alex spent the most of the last months of 1977 giving the owners of the noisiest pubs and nightclubs on Sunset Strip every last penny of their $83.83 weekly paycheck from Warners. One chilly night, the guitarist met up with the members of Angel at the notorious Rainbow Bar and Grill. Angel was a flashy glam-rock band from Washington, DC, signed to Casablanca Records as a result of another hot A&R tip from Gene Simmons. A relaxed and revived

Eddie offered his new best pals an exclusive premiere of his band's impending debut album at drummer Barry Brandt's home after the party had ended. Days later, a furious Ted Templeman called Eddie to let him know that Angel were now in the studio hastily recording their own version of "You Really Got Me," with the specific goal of gazumping Van Halen by rushing its radio release. As a result, Warners hastily produced a five-track album sampler on 12-inch vinyl (A1 "Runnin' with the Devil," A2 "Eruption," and A3 "Ice Cream Man," supported by B1 "You Really Got Me" and B2 "Jamie's Cryin'") and forced the promo EP into the hands of as many radio pluggers across the country as they could find.

On December 30 and 31, Van Halen performed two club gigs at the Whisky a Go Go to cap off a great year. When previewing the shows in the LA Times in 1978, music critic Robert Hilburn's distaste for the group was barely concealed when he wrote, "If you're still into the heavy metal sound, this is your chance to see what it looks like up close." The LA Times had previously informed readers that the band's upcoming debut long-player was set to receive "a big push" from their record label.

David Lee Roth offered an optimistic forecast while being interviewed by Raw Power at roughly the same time. The vocalist declared, "We started in the little bathroom places, and now we're at the Whisky, and we're probably gonna take over the world as soon as our record comes out."

The Pasadena quartet's debut album, Van Halen, debuted on February 10 in record stores all around the country. It starts off chaotically, as all good things should. Specifically, there is a startling, conflicting blair and whirr of car horns that evokes the claustrophobic atmosphere of a mid-afternoon traffic jam on a LA freeway during a smog-heavy day. The horns of Eddie's 1958 Volvo and Alex's Opel Kadett are mingled with the din. It seems as though a route has been cleared straight through to the Pacific Coast Highway, clear blue skies, and a world of sparkling promises, but suddenly Michael Anthony's "Runnin' with the Devil" bass line stomps in like a Toho Studios Daikaiju kicking cars over left and right. There isn't even a single peak in the rearview mirror for the next 35 minutes and 34 seconds of music.

Templeman served as Van Halen's banker to ensure that they, unlike his former charges Montrose, would secure a hit single. From the seductive "Runnin' with the Devil" to the stunning "Eruption" and the muscular cover of "You Really Got Me," through the raucous "Ain't Talkin' 'Bout Love"—a song Eddie wrote as a joke to take the piss out of punk rock—overdubbed with electric sitar—the Fast cars, loose morals, cheerleaders, cheeseburgers, cocaine, Daisy Dukes, bikinis, bongs, breaking waves, and curfew violations are all present in this soundtrack to youthful rebellion, which completely eradicates any traces of self-doubt and self-control. With their dazzling debut, Van Halen boldly stated that the 1980s would be their playground, just as the Beach Boys provided the soundtrack to American adolescence with their surf symphonies in the 1960s and the Eagles dominated the '70s with their tales of Laurel Canyon mishaps.

We celebrate all the violence and sex on television, all the rocking on the radio, the movies, the vehicles, and everything about being young, or semi-young, or young at heart. In an interview with Los Angeles underground publication Waxpaper, David Lee Roth said to Phast Phreddie Patterson. Van Halen is that.

Eddie Van Halen's breathtaking virtuosity lit up the sky, his lovely, seeming-to-come-naturally-and-utterly-electrifying playing making his band's debut record actually sing. If Roth was out there hawking an all-new American Dream to a generation ready to overindulge, it was Eddie Van Halen's playing that lit up the sky. Every bedroom guitarist had a new benchmark to aim for the instant the needle landed on the wax of Van Halen.

In their review of the album, Rolling Stone stated, "Mark my words: in three years, Van Halen is going to be fat, self-indulgent, and disgusting, and they'll follow Deep Purple and Led Zeppelin right into the toilet." They are probably going to be a major thing in the interim. The secret of Van Halen is that they don't do anything particularly novel, but they have the hormones to do it better than all those other bands that have grown big, indulgent, and repulsive.

Several riffs on this song surpass anything Aerosmith has created in years; Edward Van Halen has mastered the art of lead/rhythm guitar in the vein of Jimmy Page and Joe Walsh.

Eddie said to Steven Rosen, "All we're trying to do is bring some excitement back into rock 'n' roll." "It seems like a lot of people sound or act like they are old enough to be our daddies." They appear to have forgotten the essence of rock 'n' roll.

A few weeks later, when Van Halen toured with Journey and Ronnie Montrose, American fans would learn exactly how this transpired. The tumultuous and disastrous US tour of the Sex Pistols in January 1978 was overseen by Noel Monk, who Warners hired as the group's road manager. Those who attended the Journey/Ronnie Montrose/Van Halen concert at Chicago's Aragon Ballroom on March 3, 1978, can claim to have been among the first people outside of California to witness the new golden boys of the Golden State in action. Neal Schon, a guitarist for Journey, was curious to see if the band's new hotshot guitarist lived up to the buzz that was already surrounding him.

Schon remembered, "I had received a little red [vinyl] promotional EP three months prior to the tour starting." 'Both "Eruption" and "You Really Got Me" were written on it. As I was listening to "Eruption" while playing my guitar and using my amplifier in my bedroom, I thought, "What the fuck is this guy doing, for real?" I then went ahead and put it on my turntable. I was unable to understand it. I had been breaking things down and listening to Mahavishnu [Orchestra], among other individuals, but I just wasn't able to understand what he was doing. It made me crazy. We eventually went outside, where I got to know Ed and saw him perform flawlessly night after night. And all I can say is that I was relieved not to be trailing after him. Eddie was simply so passionate and inventive, doing things no one had ever seen before. Everyone was merely asking, "What is going on?"

Ed was a gunslinger and the new boy in the neighborhood.
For the Californian novices, the trip would prove to be an eye-opening educational experience. Less than a week later, as the

caravan approached Madison, Wisconsin, Monk received word that his boys would miss the Orpheum Theater performance because the stage couldn't support the equipment of all three bands. Marshall Berle and Monk had to act quickly, so they got their charges' permission to make alternative plans for this newly available time slot in their schedule and started calling nearby venues to see if anyone might be able to take the boys in for a special one-night-only headline performance. The managers of Madison's Shuffle Inn saw scheduling the young Californians as a fairly low-risk venture, even for a last-minute engagement, as the quartet's boisterous cover of "You Really Got Me" was worming its way up the Billboard Hot 100. Susan Masino, a writer and journalist who was at the time the associate editor of the Emerald City Chronicle, attended the event.

There must have been a thousand people in the sold-out club that night because The Shuffle only had seating for roughly 600, she recalls. "It was crazy." You had to stay put after the band took the stage. You weren't allowed to use the restroom or go to the bar for a drink. In fact, you were unable to move from where you were.

"First encountering Eddie... The first time I heard him on tape, I thought, "This is unbelievable." I questioned whether he could do that well on stage. He was also incredible. Never will I forget it. I'm still able to visualize it.

The four teenage musicians, understandably overjoyed by the response to their first headline performance outside of their home state, celebrated in classic rock 'n' roll style by destroying their lodging on the seventh level of the Madison Sheraton. They held fire extinguisher fights in the hallways, stuck frozen fish on the ceilings, and made the furniture in the rooms look like wood. At one time, Berle observed a sizable wooden table observing the laws of gravity from his bedroom window, three storeys up.

According to Masino, "Alex was going to throw a TV out the window, but someone from Journey stopped him because he said it would immediately come out of his pay cheque."
They were young people enjoying fun, Berle remarked.

As the tour went on, it became very clear to everyone in attendance that Van Halen was consistently the star of the show. Monk and Berle were repeatedly warned by Journey's 'people' that the group would be removed from the tour, citing their offstage behavior as justification. The group was eventually removed from the tour after Journey's road crew pulled the standard sabotage tricks to try to knock the newcomers off their stride - limiting the PA volume and arbitrarily shortening set times. If they had been unable to see every day that Van Halen, not the headlining act, was driving a rise in ticket sales, they might have taken the threats more seriously.

Eddie jokingly remarked to his friend Steven Rosen, "We're kicking some ass," as he learned that Van Halen will break the Billboard Top 30 the next week. "When we first started out, we were brand new; I believe our album had only been released for a week when the tour began. And right now, we're practically overtaking Journey in the charts and other things. They're panicking as a result. They could be content to get rid of us, I believe.

In the end, Van Halen performed at New York's Palladium on April 28 for the tour's final show. The quartet would have little time to consider the lessons they had learnt over the past six weeks because they would be starting a tour with Black Sabbath in Belgium the following week.

Perhaps it was inevitable that this highly calibrated machine would experience a fault sooner rather than later when operating at such a high intensity. However, nobody in the band foresaw Eddie breaking first. The band was taking advantage of some downtime in Paris after performing a triumphant headlining gig there when Noel Monk learned that Eddie wanted to return home. The musician was crying when Monk discovered him in his hotel room.

Eddie sobbed in between saying, "I don't want to be a rock star." I detest this nonsense. I simply want to return home.
Monk, who was having a hard time believing what he was hearing, comforted the guitarist but noted that the best thing Eddie could do for himself, Alex, Jan, and Eugenia was to pursue his aspirations and

achieve the success that would forever change their lives. The wager paid off. Eddie continued.

***

The heavy metal pioneers could feel their advancing years. Although Black Sabbath had planned to celebrate their tenth anniversary as a band in 1978, the band was actually disintegrating at the seams at the time.

Frontman Ozzy Osbourne said that he was finding less enjoyment in being in a rock group. "I don't think anyone was in it anymore," said the speaker.

Osbourne had formally taken a leave of absence from Sabbath in the fall of 1977 to be with his dying father Jack. However, the twenty-eight-year-old singer's disappointment and dissatisfaction with the music industry were all too evident when the New Musical Express interviewed him at his home in Staffordshire in November 1977. He was emphatic he would not be returning.

I know I've let a lot of people down, but I don't think people realize how dark my Sabbath has been through the years, he admitted.The company is in trouble. Too many people waste a lot of money by doing nothing but sitting around doing nothing. There's a lot of talent out there, but they're afraid to participate because they fear they'll wind up wearing concrete wellingtons and floating down the Thames.

"We all believed we were gods of tin." However, in the end, it did nothing more than turn around and kick us in the teeth. For a while, I just need a simple life. All I want to do is live a typical, everyday life. I'm not a can of beans that's wandering about. And I started to feel like a product, just like that. Never again will I allow myself to be a prostitute.

On January 16, 1978, Sabbath made their first appearance of the year on BBC TV's Look! Hear! program. Former Savoy Brown/Fleetwood Mac frontman Dave Walker stood between guitarist Tony Iommi and bassist Terry 'Geezer' Butler to perform the anti-war anthem 'War Pigs' and the recently written, as of yet unrecorded 'Junior's Eyes. When Osbourne unexpectedly returned to the group just before the Birmingham band left for Canada to record their eighth studio album at Toronto's Sounds Interchange Studios, it came as a real shock. As Osbourne's primary memory of his time at the facility is, "We were all fucked-up with drugs and alcohol," familiar tensions constantly resurfaced during difficult studio sessions. However, the prospect of returning to the UK for a sold-out springtime tenth-anniversary tour provided so much comfort that the four musicians could persuade themselves that their new album title, Never Say Die!, was a sincere mission statement. Ozzy Osbourne asked Sabbath's booking agency Premier Talent to find 'a bar band from LA' to open the show on their homecoming dates because the band was wary of putting too much strain on their internal engines after taking AC/DC on the road as support during their previous run of European shows and finding it difficult to match the energy levels of Malcolm and Angus Young's feral, livewire Aussies.

Even though Van Halen and Sabbath in the US shared a record company, the English quartet had not yet heard of the young American band. On the first night of the tour, May 16, at Sheffield City Hall, Osbourne, Iommi, Butler, and drummer Bill Ward sneaked out of their dressing room to see the final few songs of the Californian quartet's performance out of curiosity. Just as the group's boyish, beaming guitarist finished playing his solo showcase, "Eruption," with his fingers darting and dancing around the fretboard, and their swaggering, bare-chested blond leader gave the rhythm section the go-ahead to launch into "You Really Got Me," they made their way to the side of the stage. Sabbath silently made their way back to their dressing room.

We were sitting there exclaiming, "That was incredible." "And then it finished, and we were just too stunned to speak," Ozzy Osbourne remembered.

According to Tony Iommi, "I didn't know very much about Van Halen at all, but when I first heard them, it was like, "Bloody hell!" They had fantastic players, great energy, and catchy melodies. "Wow, blimey, these are really good!" was all we could say.

The idea of performing with Black Sabbath, according to Eddie Van Halen, first "scared the shit" out of his band; Noel Monk recalls the group as being "practically awestruck" in their company. Since they were performing as Genesis with Eddie on vocals, the Van Halen brothers have played Sabbath songs, and the guitarist regards Tony Iommi as "the master of riffs." When Eddie's awkward initial attempt to establish a rapport with Iommi backstage—referring to "the second song on side two of [Sabbath's 1971 album] Master of Reality"—was met with the imposing guitarist's chilly gaze and the confused response, "What the fuck, mate?," his nerves were barely calmed. However, the UK music press had praised Van Halen's debut album - Sounds writer Geoff Barton judged it to be a "magnificent debut" and hailed the band as "brand new heavy metal heroes" - and Sabbath's audience were warm and welcoming from the start. Even the snotty, pseudo-intelligent NME gave it a rave review by their traditional hard-rock-hating standards. Van Halen's assurance increased with each performance.

Ozzy Osbourne remembers, "They were unbelievably good." We had never heard finger-tapping music like Eddie played. He played the guitar quite well.

Geezer Butler concurs, saying, "They went over incredibly well." "The only thing that really irritated me was that they came off as a really raw band at the beginning of the tour, but as it went on, it seemed like they were sort of ripping us off." At a period when I was the only bass player who had ever used a wah pedal, Eddie's guitar solos were becoming longer, David Lee Roth was emulating everything that Ozzy would do, and the bass player even started using a wah pedal. By the time we took the stage, most folks said, "Oh, I've already seen all this." We appeared to be our own tribute group. We weren't too concerned about it because they were all pretty nice guys, but Tony had to tell Eddie to "behave yourself" in a few words.

They observed us from the side of the stage virtually every night, according to Iommi, and undoubtedly learned from us by observing what worked and what energized the audience. However, it seemed a

26

little off when we entered the stage since we appeared to be copying what they were doing.

I asked Eddie one night, "Hey, Eddie, are you gonna play a couple of tracks off our new album tomorrow?" I then brought him into my room and told him, "You can't be doing the same sort of thing on the same show."

Eddie was a fantastic guitarist who had undoubtedly grown up listening to other guitarists. However, he had developed his own style. Most evenings, he would stop by my room or I would go to his, and we would talk all night as we smoked a little coke. I grew to really admire him as a player and he became a really good buddy. I'm really grateful they were there because it helped me find a lifelong buddy.

Before their performance at Aberdeen's Capitol Theatre on May 19, four dates into the tour, Van Halen learned that their album had surpassed the 500,000-sale threshold in the US, earning the band their first gold record. They celebrated by getting extremely wasted on Glenmorangie whiskey and, in time-honored style, decorating their lodging with their specialized interior design abilities.

Eddie said with a hint of guilt, "We wrote our logo on the walls with shoe polish." The police arrived the following morning and led us out of the nation—not because we trashed their hotel, but rather because one of our team members had taken a pillow! They led us all the way to the border and warned us, "Don't ever come back." We were all terrified to death!

Roth soberly remarked, "A gold record was only division finals." "Was success even if you had a gold record if you weren't on the radio or television?" We lacked a reliable method for measuring our success. The intellectual elite did not accept us. Those in the know, and especially the UK press, were enthused about Elvis Costello and The Clash at the time because they were legitimate rivals. However, it provided an excuse for a blowout in a peaceful hotel.

Tony Iommi invited his close friend Brian May from Queen to join him at the side of the stage to observe the talented Californians in action when the tour stopped at London's Hammersmith Odeon.

The two of us saw Eddie Van Halen perform, and it was absolutely wonderful, almost too glorious to take in, May recalled. To witness this man bouncing around with a guitar like a kitten, carrying it to unimaginable places Since Jimi Hendrix, there has not been anything as stunning.

Photographer Ross Halfin, a contributor to the magazine Sounds, was also present that evening with plans to capture the performance.
Before the Hammersmith concert, Halfin saw them perform in Lewisham, an unfashionable south London borough. At the conclusion of their set, David Lee Roth shook up two champagne bottles and shouted, "Lewisham, this is the rock 'n' roll capital of the fucking world, man!" Halfin remembers this as being hilarious. When we arrived at Hammersmith, Van Halen had a PR girl from Warners in LA with them named Heidi Robinson, and she insisted that she had to approve every photographer who was going to shoot them. At the time, photographers could typically shoot whatever they wanted, especially when it came to opening bands. Even though I did take some photos from the balcony, we all just started giggling and refused to take pictures. In retrospect, that was a very clever approach to sell them. They appeared to be quite elusive and exclusive.

When Van Halen performed, Malcolm Dome, a music critic for Record Mirror at the time, recalled, "The place was packed for them." Everyone wanted to see them because they had already generated a lot of interest among metalheads and other individuals who frequently purchased rock records from abroad. They were unquestionably superior to Sabbath that evening. Van Halen were so thrilling, bright, dynamic, and innovative in contrast to the sloppy Sabbath. They aged the Sabbath. One could not help but think, "This is amazing." They had a futuristic sound.

In actuality, Van Halen started to emphasize this point in each interview. The trio recorded their first-ever TV interview for the

Australia Broadcasting Corporation's renowned Countdown show in London's Soho Square the afternoon before their performance at the Hammersmith Odeon. Eddie firmly asserted, "The '60s are over, and so are the '70s," while gazing directly into the camera when the interviewer claimed that hard rock was seeing an unexpected rebirth. The new thing is us.

During a quick eight-date tour of Japan the next week, Van Halen made their debut on Japanese television, and Roth declared them to be "the future of rock 'n' roll for the United States and for the world." This mission statement was further elaborated in a full-page advertisement placed by Warners in the June 3 issue of the US trade publication Billboard: The inscription said, "This is the start of something big," referencing the album's achievement in the Top 30 in France, Australia, and Japan. It's obvious that the world adores Van Halen.

Domestic matters, however, took precedence for the time being. Following their final Japanese performance in Osaka's Cultural Hall on June 27, the band traveled to Dallas, Texas, for the first-ever Texxas Jam, which would be their greatest performance to date. En route, they stopped in Tokyo's recently constructed Narita airport and Los Angeles. A line-up that included Aerosmith, Ted Nugent, Heart, Journey, Frank Marino and Mahogany Rush, among others, had almost 100,000 people paying $12.50 a person... and Van Halen discovered that practically all of their equipment had vanished between Osaka and Texas when they got on the scene. Unsurprisingly, Noel Monk was furious after hearing the news, as photographer Neil Zlozower, who had been recruited by the promoter to capture the event, would later learn to his detriment.

He explains, "Me and another photographer got hired by the promoter to shoot the festival. We had access to film all the bands for their whole set; back then, they didn't have that "first three songs only" garbage that they have now. As I waited for them to take the platform, a little man wearing black leather gloves, a black leather coat, and Peter Fonda Easy Rider sunglasses approaches and asks, "What the fuck are you doing on my stage?" He is undoubtedly the scariest man I have ever seen. Noel Monk was there. My response is,

"I'm shooting Van Halen." And he responded, "No, you're not; leave my stage immediately." I countered, "But we're doing it for the promoter!" And he responded, "Yeah, you're doing everybody else for the promoter but Van Halen." He was quite violent, and I muttered to myself, "I don't want to argue with this fucking guy, he looks like he means business." Therefore, I thought, "OK, I'll go out and watch this band to see if they deliver the goods." And, holy crap, Van Halen were fucking incredible and amazing. I believe many attendees left that festival with a new favorite band.

Van Halen made their way back to California on July 9 for what was supposed to be their largest headlining performance to date at Long Beach Arena. The LA Times' top music critic Robert Hilburn, who had previously written negatively about the band's chances after their sold-out two-night performance at the Whisky a Go Go to end 1977, was assigned to cover the quartet's official return.

David Roth was ecstatic, Hilburn reported in his article, which was printed in the newspaper on July 11. The lead vocalist of the Pasadena-based band, who is 22 years old, wouldn't take the stage at the Long Beach Arena for another three hours, but the tension was building. He had been anticipating this performance for years.

Van Halen has finally graduated to the big time after a protracted apprenticeship in the taverns, little clubs, and other stops on the neighborhood rock back streets.After the sound check, the long-haired, slim Roth said, "This is really special." We last performed in Los Angeles on New Year's Eve at the Whisky. It resembles our return home. Since February, we have been on the road, and now we have our first gold record. What better setting for a celebration?

We believed we could succeed as soon as we got going. We believed, 'We're cool now, and we're going to be cooler.'
Eddie's post-performance celebration was marred a little by a fight with the venue's security. The guitarist had returned from Japan with gifts for his family, so after the concert he asked his buddy Wally Olney to help him transport the items from the band's tour bus to his father's vehicle. Eddie was besieged by well-wishers as he made his way back to the auditorium; some of them were pleading with him

for passes so they could gain entry to the location and attend the after-show party. One of the venue's security officers noticed the ruckus and stepped in to demand that the crowd leave the area right away.

Eddie retorted, "I'm in the band and I'm going back in."
No, you're not.
Punches were thrown during the guard's effort to drag the guitarist out of the backstage area.

You scumbag! You're in serious trouble, man! After spitting, Eddie retreated and pushed his way into the arena. A short while later, Marshall Berle led his guitarist and the show's promoter back into the parking lot. The security guard's position was immediately terminated when Eddie revealed the security goon who had attempted to have him expelled.

The rest of the year's Van Halen tour schedule reads like a wet fantasy for a hard-rock aficionado. The band performed at the Superdome in New Orleans on July 13 in support of the Rolling Stones and the Doobie Brothers. After 48 hours, the group performed at Kansas City, Missouri's Royals Stadium's Summer Jam alongside Steve Miller Band, Kansas, and Eddie Money. Two days later, they performed in front of an estimated 25,000 people on Credit Island, near Davenport, Iowa, at the Mississippi River Jam as the opening act for the Doobie Brothers, the Atlanta Rhythm Section, and their old friends Journey. They returned to California, including the San Francisco Bay Area, a week later, on July 23, for the sixth annual Bill Graham's Day on the Green celebration at the Oakland Coliseum. The concert, which was the third of five one-day events marketed under the Day on the Green label that summer, included Aerosmith and Foreigner as co-headliners, AC/DC as the day's opening act, and Van Halen between them and Canadian guitar hero Pat Travers. Eddie went to the side of the stage before his band's performance to check out Malcolm and Angus Young's band.

He recalled, "AC/DC was probably one of the most intense live bands I've ever seen in my life." "We have to follow these motherfuckers?" I was wondering as I stood on the edge of the stage.

If the guitarist was intimidated, it didn't come out in his playing. Joe Perry, the guitarist for Aerosmith, was admiring Van Halen from the side stage.

We arrived early because, according to Perry, "it was an amazing bill" and we wanted to watch all those bands. The first Van Halen album, in my opinion, was fantastic. I remember listening to it and thinking, "Wow, these guys are steamrolling, man!" It was the kind of music that you could be sure would be popular in a stadium. They most definitely lived up to it while performing live. David Lee Roth was one of the best live frontmen I've ever seen, and Eddie altered how people perceived guitar playing. I like rock 'n' roll, and I recall that being one of the performances that lived up to the hype.
Eddie made the decision to shoot some hoops in the backstage area while he relaxed following the performance. He chose Guitar Player journalist Jas Obrecht to be his opponent in a one-on-one match.

Obrecht relates, "This kid comes up to me, incredibly ripped and muscular, and says, "Hey, man, can I shoot baskets with you?" 'I responded, "Sure." So we engaged in a fifteen minute one-on-one game where he proved to be really skilled and even defeated me. He was swift and possessed a hook shot that I was unable to stop. He asked us as we sat down to relax at the edge of the tiny court, "Hey, what band are you in?" Then I say, "I'm not in a band." "Well, what are you doing here?" he asks. I introduced myself and stated, "I'm here from Guitar Player magazine to interview Pat Travers, but Travers blew me off." "Travers blew you off?," he asked. That is so incredibly unbelievable. Why don't you ask me a question? I had never been interviewed before. "Well, who are you?" I ask. He introduced himself as Edward Van Halen and said, "I'm Edward Van Halen." A light then appeared, saying, "Of course!"

The young musician, whose model Obrecht couldn't identify, fiddled with his instrument as they conversed. It was a replica of a Fender Stratocaster, according to Van Halen, who said that it was his own DIY invention. Reject components from emerging Californian guitar maker Charvel were used in its construction.

He said, "I paid $50 for the body and $80 for the neck and installed a vintage Gibson PAF pickup that was rewound to my specifications." I've done a lot of experimentation with the one-pickup sound because I like it. A sound that is bad for rhythm is produced when the pickup is placed too far forward or too closely to the bridge. I prefer it farther back because it gives the sound a little more bite and edge. I also used huge Gibsons to install my own frets. Everything is controlled by a single volume knob. No fancy tone knobs are used by me. Give me one knob, that's all. I see so many people with these advanced guitars with numerous switches, equalizers, and treble enhancers. It sounds cool and is easy.

Obrecht claims, "I held his guitar and I immediately noticed three things." One was that the neck was wider than it typically was; it resembled the width of a classical guitar. The second was that Eddie had made the nut by the headstock extra wide so you could actually grab the A-string or D-string and move it around inside the opening. He did this because he was so aggressive with the whammy bar and needed to do something to prevent it from going out of tune. The third point was how homemade it appeared to be. It appeared to be what it was: a body that a child had used woodworking tools on, painted with bicycle spray paint in his parents' garage. Although it appeared to be a cheap instrument, the sound that came from it was absolutely incredible.

The Frankenstrat appeared to be barely controlled anarchy, as Rolling Stone reporter Brian Hiatt afterwards observed.
Obrecht praised the young guitarist for his role in igniting the modern rock movement when he and Van Halen parted ways.
Van Halen declared, "I have never given up on rock." There are many who used to declare, "Bullshit, that rock is dead and gone."
The group reunited with Black Sabbath on August 22 to embark on their US tour. It was obvious to everyone present that Sabbath were being murdered every night; the promoters should have also engaged a crime scene investigator to chronicle the tour and mark the location with chalk.

Geezer Butler recalls, "The record company was all over Van Halen." Van Halen had all the star treatment from the record business since they were already of the opinion that we were outdated and past our prime. By contrast, we received nothing. We attended a reception at Warner Brothers when the Never Say Die! a record was released, and they were playing Bob Marley's CD without recognizing us! I believe they were about to drop us because of the decline in our sales.

After a few beers, I recall being in a hotel room in San Diego with Geezer and a record label representative. One of us reportedly stated to the latter, "Be honest, you're only using us on this tour to promote Van Halen, aren't you?" He continued, "You're right." Additionally, if your record label won't support you, You either say, "Right, we're going to go out there and fucking show them how to do it," or you just give up when a band performs before you and does better than you. They also had years on us, and after battling this legal battle with our former manager for years, I was simply fucking exhausted. We never intended to become accountants or lawyers when we joined a band, but that is exactly how it turned out. We were completely clueless.

The members of Thin Lizzy, Phil Lynott, Scott Gorham, and Gary Moore, who were on a brief club tour with AC/DC in the Midwest, saw the Pasadena band's performance at Detroit's Cobo Hall on September 14 while they had some free time.

"Wow, man, I was just out with Van Halen - what a fucking band!" was a common refrain anytime we hung out with anyone from the label when we were on the same American record label, Warners. Gorham, a guitarist from California, recalls. 'When this happened, Phil eventually started admonishing them, saying, "Look, if you get into this fucking car, you're not going to talk about Van Halen, all right?" We were therefore curious about this band that we had heard so much about. And then these lads appeared and shredded everyone like a fresh asshole. They were incredible. I asked Gary, "What the heck is that? when Eddie started performing his tapping thing. What's he doing there, exactly? He only stared at Gary before he responded, "I don't know." When I went to ask Gary another question ten minutes later, he had already left. He said, "Hey, check this out," and he began tapping away as I stood in his hotel room the following day. The previous evening, he returned to the hotel to teach himself how to do it.

On September 22, UK music journalist Sylvie Simmons caught up with the tour in Fresno, California, and she too fell in love with the vivacious young Californians.

Sabbath are difficult to match for pure crowd-pleasing, Simmons wrote in Sounds, or they would be if a group like Van Halen weren't around. They resemble Sabbath in some ways, but younger and without the embalmed appearance from ten years ago. Dave Lee Roth, who is louder and bigger, must be the rock scene's most enthusiastic frontman right now. His jeans have larger flares even than usual. You must watch his jack-knife leaps from the drum set to believe them. Wows, pings, and squeals are interspersed throughout his singing. He makes brazen interlude speeches, such as "Fresno, the rock 'n' roll capital of the world?" C'mon! The ladies just swarm around him. The majority of the women in this predominantly male audience appear to have pushed their way to the stage's front and are grasping his legs. The remaining members of the band are traditional rock heroes who are really talented musicians.

Runnin' with the Devil, Jamie's Cryin', Feel Your Love, Ain't Talkin' 'Bout Love, and the quartet's set-closing cover of "You Really Got Me"—"a really macho, suggestive version of the Kinks' classic that has the audience going wild"—were among the songs Simmons singled out as highlights.

Other than the self-assured Sabs, she concluded, "any other band would refuse to follow this group." They perform that well live. Ozzy Osbourne told Simmons later that evening in a hotel bar in the city, to the accompaniment of a jazz trio playing Barry Manilow songs, "Van Halen are one of the most high-energy trips I've seen in America in years." They are fantastic. When I see David up there, it's like seeing a younger version of myself. You know, when I was 21? All I can do is hope that they endure for as long as we have.

Twenty-four hours later, Van Halen made their largest and most audacious move of the year when they joined Sammy Hagar,

Sabbath, and headliners Boston at Summerfest at Anaheim Stadium. Four parachutists spilled out of a plane that was circling over the stadium as opening act Hagar left the stage. Audience members saw that each parachute bore the Van Halen emblem as they got closer to the ground. Van Halen entered the stadium, the venue PA proclaimed, "from out of the sky!" As soon as the skydivers landed in the backstage area, Roth, Anthony, and the Van Halen brothers came onto the stage wearing similar jumpsuits, drawing wildly enthusiastic cheers. You only get one chance to create a good first impression, they say.

Robert Hilburn, writing for the LA Times, had to admit that the group was "hard to resist for anyone with a tolerance for hard-driving, assaultive rock," and he came to the conclusion that the hometown heroes "could well be the heir apparent to Aerosmith's hard-rock American crown."

When the band's debut album broke the one million sales threshold in the US on October 10, 1978, they were back in Europe on their first headlining tour. Each band member received a custom-made VH platinum necklace from Marshall Berle, who ultimately charged them separately for the price of production.

On December 3, Van Halen's first world tour came to an end in San Diego. The group then took a five-day break at the Club Med resort in Cancun, Mexico. The band got a party invitation from their record label back in Los Angeles. Given that the quartet's debut record had reached two million US sales, Warners intended to give them platinum discs. The event was held in LA's only all-nude strip bar, the Body Shop on Sunset Boulevard. Marshall Berle's uncle Milton served as the emcee, and visitors included Stevie Nicks and Bonnie Raitt. However, their contract required the delivery of a second album within a year of the release of their debut, as well as the settlement of a sizable debt, so the hungover band was back in Sunset Sound the next day with Ted Templeman.

"Let me get this straight," I said to Ted. We traveled for a year and sold two million records, but we still owe you $2 million." Alex Van

36

Halen questioned in astonishment. Simply shrugging, Templeman sent the drummer back into the live room.

Boys,   welcome   to   the   music   industry...

Chapter 3: Defeat of Control

No one in Van Halen could have been unaware that the proposal they were being asked to consider was, by the letter of the law, illegal as they listened to Noel Monk detail exactly how, where, and why their money was going to be spent. The practice of "payola," in which powerful people at radio stations are offered money, gifts, vacations, drugs, or sexual favors in exchange for airplay, may have been as well-established as the music business itself, but just because everyone else engaged in it or chose to ignore it when it was authorized on their behalf, it didn't make the behavior any less deplorable. The phrase "direct payment evil" was originally used by the entertainment industry publication Variety in a front-page editorial denouncing the practice in 1916.

The decision to be made, however, seemed like a no-brainer to the attentive band members as Van Halen's manager patiently explained that in the considered and trusted opinion of Warner Bros. Records, offering financial inducements to selected radio stations for guaranteed airtime was the only realistic option now available to them. David Lee Roth, in Monk's memory, gave the group's approval for the action plan. More than anybody else, Roth was aware of the importance of perception in the music industry. The idea that Van Halen might be perceived as being on the decline after just three years in the spotlight was inconceivable, unthinkable. The industry placed a huge premium on forward momentum—rising chart positions, swelling box-office receipts, deeper penetration on the radio, promotion to magazine front covers.

After a contentious discussion between Noel Monk and Carl Scott, head of artist development at Warners, the emergency band meeting was called. While the group's third album, Women and Children First, and its predecessor, Van Halen II, both sold one million copies in the United States within three months of being published, Fair Warning, the group's fourth album, which was released on April 29 1981, had only just surpassed the half-million mark by mid-summer Due to Ted Templeman's support, Van Halen had become accustomed to being seen and treated as a priority act by Warners from the beginning. However, if they were shown to be unable to keep up with the label's top acts, they ran the risk of losing their priority position. In his novel Runnin' with the Devil, Monk revisits the conversation with Scott and recalls asking, "Isn't there something we can do?" and hearing the response, "Yeah, there is." But it's not inexpensive.

Ironically, Fair Warning was a greater album than the two collections that came before it, pound for pound. However, it lacked a smash song, was darker and heavier, and at times was difficult to listen to. From the jaw-dropping tapped intro of album opener "Mean Street" to the gritty synth rumbles supporting set closer "One Foot Out the Door," which was written in the tumultuous, stressful winter months before the guitarist and his fiancée were due to marry, a time Eddie later remembered as "a dark period," this album was unquestionably also Eddie Van Halen's.

Steven Rosen was told by Eddie that "I worked my ass off." "I came up with every idea on it in less than two weeks." I was 125 pounds, and I lost a lot of weight and sleep because I knew I had to do it.
Valerie Bertinelli recalled, already concerned about how little time she was getting to spend with a fiancée she hardly knew, that "Ed typically worked all night in the back bedroom, where he'd set up his equipment, or at a studio in Hollywood." He experimented with ideas while seated next to his engineer until he either achieved the desired results or ran out of alcohol, cocaine, energy, inspiration, or all of the above.

Eddie admitted to Jas Obrecht, "I'm pretty much a loner." I'm just not good at getting along with others. They fail to comprehend me. Nothing to say, I suppose. I play my guitar by myself quite a bit. Just more satisfying all around.

"I need to think of something different in order for me to... I have to spend two or three hours completely alone, playing my guitar. It is quite similar to meditation. I enter a mental space where I'm not consciously considering writing.

The guitarist mostly decided not to exhume material from earlier demos, with the exception of 'Mean Street,' which borrowed from the unreleased 'Voodoo Queen' and 'She's the Woman.' He was determined to move the group forward and challenge himself as a composer and musician. Fair Warning therefore sounds thrillingly strange in several places. Dub reggae, bubbling funk, and one of Eddie's wildest solos in his career—a jazz-fusion improvisation evoking Allan Holdsworth—are all combined in the song "Push Comes to Shove." Superficially jaunty and upbeat, 'So This Is Love?' shows its dark underbelly in Roth's bitter lyric ('The grass is never greener, and there's plenty around'), the prom-queen-turned-porn-queen-themed 'Dirty Movies' ladles a futuristic new-wave synth sheen atop a filthy boogie, and the swampy, oppressively heavy instrumental 'Sunday Afternoon in the Park', written on an Electro-Harmonix Mini-Synthesizer, sounds like a 1970s Italian horror theme. Eddie said that she was the inspiration for it, saying, "It's us fighting all the time."

The album's versatility and innovation make the more "traditional" tracks even more powerful. With its ferocious riff, stacked vocal harmonies, and a song about freedom and life's limitless possibilities, "Unchained" may be the quintessential Van Halen rock song and, in Eddie's words, "a blazer." I really like that music, he said. It's unusual for me to listen to a recording of my own playing and experience goosebumps, but that is one of them. Famously, David Lee Roth breaks the fourth wall in the song by yelling, "One break, coming up!" in response to an exhausted-sounding Ted Templeman appealing, "Come on, Dave, gimme a break!"

In a candid interview with Steven Rosen for Guitar World, Eddie stated, "The truth is, I don't think he sang as good as I played," before launching into an out-of-character rebuttal of the notion that Van Halen was a cohesive group.

At least, the guitarist said, Dave "pulls his weight." Mike Anthony doesn't, it seems. He has no influence at all and does nothing. Period. But with the money he made from us, he completely renovated his home and bought a [Porsche] Turbo Carrera for himself. Whatever.'

Eddie revealed further by saying, "I wasn't very happy with the way things were going or the way people were approaching the entire recording process." I would slip back into the studio at four in the morning with the engineer, Donn Landee, and completely redo all the solos and overdubs to my specifications. The awful thing was that nobody even paid attention. That is how disinterested they were musically.

It was difficult to ignore the guitarist's boldness and command of the performance. J. D. Considine's assessment of the album, which was published in the October issue of Musician, was the most analytical and perceptive.

Whereas earlier albums focused more on strength than intellect, Fair Warning achieves an outstanding balance of musical sophistication and aural excess. Make yourself a cup of tea and turn on Genesis if increasing gentility is what you're after. On the other hand, if you prefer hard rock that presumes its audience is more intelligent than the typical lap dog, this is the record for you.

Despite all the stress, anxiety, and uncertainty that went into the campaign, Fair Warning's promotional cycle came to a magnificent conclusion. The tour came to an end on October 24 and 25, 1981, when the quintet supported the Rolling Stones, who were then approaching their 30th anniversary and were still the biggest rock band in the world, at the Tangerine Bowl in Orlando, Florida. Although Van Halen had quickly matured over the course of the preceding 12 months, their naivety having long ago been destroyed, they weren't yet so cynical as to dismiss this as merely another weekend. Post-soundcheck, looking out over the empty stadium, America's loudest and brastiest band fell into awed stillness and humbly bent their heads when Mick Jagger approached. Noel Monk observed, "It was like God himself had entered our midst."

When Eddie looked up, Jagger was staring directly in his direction. He remarked, "You are a fucking brilliant guitar player, Edward," saying as much.

***

Pete Angelus started to worry that he had lost control on the set of the video shoot for Van Halen's cover of Roy Orbison's "(Oh) Pretty Woman" when the dwarves began giving magic mushrooms to the cast and crew. In a hypothetical fantasy piece he had submitted to Warners, the band's lighting director and creative adviser, Angelus, had the quartet save a damsel in distress from the grasp of terrible monsters. Angelus made a compelling case that the campy, lighthearted, and purposefully corny campaign would solidify the band's reputation as everyone's favorite naughty-but-nice all-American rock gods.

Van Halen, like many of its hard-rock contemporaries, initially discounted the importance of music videos. Even though it hadn't been under the consideration of their idols, the Beatles, the Rolling Stones, the Who, or Queen, most rock bands tended to view shooting promotional films as a waste of time, money, and energy prior to MTV's inception on August 1, 1981. While Warners had commissioned videos for "Runnin' with the Devil," "Jamie's Cryin'," and "You Really Got Me" as part of the promotion for Van Halen's debut album, the three clips were secured in a single day of filming at the Whisky a Go Go, and their influence was regarded as negligible in the album's subsequent success, especially when weighed against the indisputable value of radio airplay and the word-of-mouth buzz It seemed prudent to invest a little more time, creativity, and imagination into the video, not least because MTV's influence on the record-buying public was obviously becoming increasingly significant. However, the cover of "(Oh) Pretty Woman" was envisaged as a stand-alone single, a stopgap release to buy the band some downtime following their six months on the road promoting Fair Warning. As a result, Pete Angelus' storyboard was completely Van Halenized and filled with sarcastic, ironic touches.

The band made the decision to dress up as different characters for reasons that are best known to them: Roth was to dress as Napoleon Bonaparte, Eddie would portray a cowboy, Alex would adopt a Tarzan look, and Michael Anthony would dress as a samurai warrior. The decision was subsequently made to cast transgender performer International Chrysis, two dwarfs, a hunchback, and other significant supporting characters. The on-set catering was designed to be primarily beer, cannabis, Jack Daniel's, and cocaine; hallucinogenic mushrooms were an added bonus. It was all fun and games until Angelus lost his dwarfs, when two cameramen left the scene due to heavy intoxication.

Accuse Roth. It was Roth who pushed the group to record a cover version in order to maintain a presence in the market during what was meant to be a lengthy sabbatical. Roth was twitching with nervous energy as the post-tour withdrawal symptoms began to set in at the end of 1981. The vocalist actually requested that a remake of the 1964 smash hit "Dancing in the Street" by Martha and the Vandellas be recorded, but Eddie chose Roy Orbison's seven-million-selling song from the same year instead. The group went back to Sunset Sound Studio with Ted Templeman and recorded three songs in one day: the single A-side, the enduring live favorite "Happy Trails," which was written by Roy Rogers and his wife Dale Evans and is instantly recognizable as the theme song for their long-running radio/TV show. They also tracked the dense instrumental "Intruder," which was needed to fill out the soundtrack for the video. The idea was to release the song into the market after the accompanying video was finished, and then gradually pull the band back into the background for a well-deserved break.

But when mankind creates plans, God chuckles. Radio jumped on the bubbly, energizing cover even as MTV recoiled at the video's joyous political incorrectness and yanked it from daily play within weeks after receiving hundreds of complaints. Mo Ostin and Lenny Waronker at Warner Bros. approached Ted Templeman to demand the release of a new full-length Van Halen album within weeks as the song accelerated up the Billboard Hot 100 list, where it would peak at number 12 in mid-April 1982—exactly what the band didn't want.

The quartet reluctantly gave in to the pressure, negotiating a compromise with their employers: they would release a new record, but since they had no time to write new songs and were once more curiously reluctant to delve too deeply into their vault of unreleased material, it would heavily rely on cover songs to capture the raw energy of their unexpected hit single. Sunset Sound was booked, so the band was moved to Warners' Amigo Studios, where Templeman and Landee cut the record in just twelve days.

Reviewers weren't blind to the fact that the entire album clocks in at just over 31 minutes in length, testing the notion of "long-player."
In Creem, Jeffrey Morgan wrote, "This album is an exceptionally vicious kick in the teeth to Van Halen fans everywhere; fans who - by buying their albums, attending their concerts, and wearing their merchandise - have made David Lee Roth, Alex Van Halen, Eddie Van Halen, and Michael Anthony millionaires."

This allusion to the conflicts inside the band was most definitely not an ill-advised slip of the tongue, given Roth's keen awareness of the Fourth Estate's workings. A fan might have thought the group was closer than ever after hearing the quartet giggle through the four-part harmony a cappella vocals on "Happy Trails" or hear Eddie and Alex's clarinet-playing father Jan trill throughout "Big Bad Bill," but this was only a fantasy. And a frustrated Eddie would get tired of twisting the truth very quickly.

Later in 1982, when speaking about his most recent solo effort, "Cathedral," he revealed to longtime friend Jas Obrecht that guitarist Eddie had originally intended to include the song on a previous album but had been overridden by Roth, who reportedly told him frankly, "Fuck this, man." No more guitar solos, please."

Eddie said, "He's on an ego trip." "He always has been." Ted was unaware that Dave felt that way. When Dave wasn't in the studio one day, I asked Ted, "What do you think of this? What do you think of that, then? I played him the intro to "Little Guitars," the brief flamenco-sounding passage, and "Cathedral," and he exclaimed, "God! Why the fuck didn't you demonstrate this to me sooner? Then I told him, "Dave just said, 'Fuck the guitar hero shit, you know, we're a band.'" Ted thus exclaimed, "Fuck Dave." Therefore, we wore it nevertheless.

Although he didn't confront Templeman with the same venom, Eddie was also furious with the producer because, in his opinion, the producer "wasted" a keyboard riff by layering it over the "Dancing in

44

the Street" theme rather than using it to create a Peter Gabriel-inspired composition. Eddie was never the confrontational kind, so he sulked instead of rejecting the concept, but the event still bothered him.

The amusingly named Hide Your Sheep tour, also known as the Kicking Ass and Taking Names tour, was initially planned to run for eighty concerts across North America, commencing on July 14 in Augusta, Georgia. Its purpose was to cover up the cracks that were starting to threaten the group's foundation. In actuality, it merely served to heighten the band's already-existing conflicts between the frontman and the band's composer. When the caravan arrived in California in September, Eddie took a break from the humid environment to visit his friends in Kiss, who were working as a trio at the Record Plant Studio to record what would become their Creatures of the Night album after troubled guitarist Ace Frehley left. It's unclear what exactly happened that afternoon in the fall, but Gene Simmons continues to stand by his claim that Eddie got so tired of working with David Lee Roth that he offered to leave his own band in order to fill Kiss's open guitar position.

When this writer inquired about this rumor with Paul Stanley, he confirmed that Eddie did visit Kiss in the recording studio. "I remember him listening to the solo for "Creatures of the Night," which he thought was amazing," he remembered. However, he had no recollection of any conversation with the guitarist or even his louder-than-life bassist about Eddie joining the New York band. Stanley was adamant that this did not happen when it was claimed that, had Van Halen genuinely made an offer to join the band during his powwow with Simmons, one would have envisioned the bassist bringing up the subject when he returned to the studio.

The ambassador said, "You'll have to make of that what you will."

Alex had, in fact, talked Eddie out of leaving their band just one year earlier, something that nobody outside of their closest and most trusted pals knew.

The drummer admitted, "Things got a little loopy in 1981 when Ed got married to Valerie." He was receiving unwanted press, and the situation got out of hand. Ed wished to give up. We've invested too much time in this to give it up, I informed him. Even though the image and words may be improved, people are still hearing your song. Hey, we're playing, I exclaimed. Every musician aspires to achieve that.

Regardless of the facts, the Hide Your Sheep tour continued, with the exception of three New Jersey gigs in October that were canceled after another controversial incident in which the guitarist fractured his wrist after punching a wall in rage. Eddie found the opportunity to contribute to Michael Jackson's impending Thriller album later that month, once he had fully recovered. He dropped by Westlake Recording Studios in Los Angeles to add a guitar solo to the song "Beat It" as a favor to producer Quincy Jones.

Eddie remembered, "Michael left to go across the hall to do some children's speaking records." I believe it to have been E.T. So I enquired, "What do you want me to do?" to Quincy. Afterward, he says, "Whatever you want to do." "Be careful when you say that," I then caution. When you say, "Do whatever you want,' be careful if you know anything about me.

Jones insisted, "I'm not going to sit here and try to tell you what to play." "What you do play is the reason you are here,"

I listened to the song and asked, "Can I change some parts?" right away. Eddie recalled. As soon as I turned to face the engineer, I said, "OK, from the breakdown, chop in this part, go to this piece, pre-chorus, to the chorus, out." He put it together in about ten minutes. I then started improvising two solos over it.

Van Halen wasn't originally aware that Jackson had returned to the booth to check out his part because he was so engrossed in the music when recording the second of these solos.

'"Look, I changed the middle section of your song," I remarked,' Eddie recounted. "Now, in my opinion, he will either have his bodyguards eject me for travesting his song or he will find it amusing. He then turned to me and said, "Wow, thank you so much for having the passion to not just come in and blaze a solo, but to actually care about the song, and make it better." So I guess he gave it a listen.

Eddie left his meeting with the King of Pop without even requesting a session fee or any royalties on the song. More importantly, he didn't bother to tell his bandmates, manager, or record label about his intention to perform as a guest on the album, or even stop to think for a second that it might have been polite to do so.

Future Adele/Foo Fighters producer Greg Kurstin was a member of Dweezil's band, which entered a high school talent competition. Their rock-star coach showed up to offer his support and gave the youngster a brand-new Kramer Explorer guitar. After the performance, the guitarist met up with his teenage friends in an alleyway behind the school building for a debriefing and a smoke.

Scott Marshall, the bassist for the group, recalled: "I remember that a teacher came up and saw us all in the alley." "What are you kids doing back here?" she asks. Eddie popped out of his Porsche 930 Turbo and joked, "Gettin' high!" She panicked and bolted. She apparently didn't get the joke.

Chapter 4: Love Enters

On December 31, 1984, MTV is broadcasting live from New York City the 4th Annual New Year's Eve Rock 'N Roll Ball. Joan Jett, a former Runaways guitarist, will perform live on television with the Blackhearts. Whoopi Goldberg, Frankie Goes to Hollywood, Duran Duran, and UB40 are among the performers scheduled to appear during the four-hour show. MTV's star VJ Martha Quinn and 'Diamond' will co-host. A projected 42 million "screaming, beady-eyed, slack-jawed, drooling party monsters" will watch the video for David Lee Roth's debut solo single, "California Girls" at its world premiere.

"Edward, Alex, Michael, and the rest of the Van Halen traveling circus and animal act tonight bring a message to all of you," Roth tells the excited studio audience while looking dapper in a black tuxedo, white bow tie, red and white gloves, and white-rimmed sunglasses. "Tonight is a great moment for everyone to set their resolutions for the new year... And midnight is approaching quickly. Rock enthusiasts, you already know that it's a dog-eat-dog world out there, so it's time to choose whether you want to be a hot dog or a tiny wiener.

Roth says, "I have decided to stay a little wiener for one more year." Enjoy yourselves, baby!
As the first studio guest of the 1985 television season on David Letterman's talk show Late Night with..., Roth repeated the quip on network television on January 2. You're doing solo work, right? Letterman casually inquired after playing a clip from the "California Girls" video and asking Roth to confirm or refute some wild claims from a recently released unofficial Van Halen book. Does this portend the band's impending dissolution?

"No, no, no... " Roth remonstrated.
That occurs, you know," Letterman added.
That does occur, Roth acknowledged. The Spinal Tap narrative goes like this. No, I still have very strong tribal instincts. We'll start

fighting again in the studio in the middle of this month, and we'll release another record later this year. I hope that...

Van Halen's 1984 spent its fifty-first week on the Billboard 200 chart, peaking at number 39. With over five million copies sold, it was America's sixth-best-selling album of 1984. Roth's rendition of "California Girls" debuted on the Billboard Hot 100 two weeks later, in the week ending on January 19. It peaked on the chart on March 2 at number 3, behind REO Speedwagon's "Can't Fight This Feeling" and Wham!'s top-charting single "Careless Whisper" (credited to "Wham! featuring George Michael").

Even though he was overjoyed, Roth rejected any notion that this success may prompt him to leave Van Halen, declaring himself to be "perfectly content" with the group. Simply put, he said, "There just isn't enough time in a Van Halen day for me to sing and dance as much as I want." "I saw it as a chance to kind of spread my wings in directions the Van Halen band won't go," the singer said.

I'm not traveling alone. I'm prepared to rejoin those guys in the studio and try to talk my way back into the Top 10.

Roth acknowledged that relationships within Van Halen had evolved over time, but he did it with a wink and a smile.

He admitted to journalist Ben Fong-Torres of the San Francisco Chronicle, "Right now, in real life, I never see Edward." He doesn't call me, and I never call him. We get along wonderfully on the road. Then, we are engaged in something mutual. Fine in the studio. In the workplace? Roth shrugged without emotion. 'Eh.
Conflicts related to business. Different people are affected differently by our money and power. We experience a significant swell when we aren't moving forward; when everyone has had some time to reflect on their situation, they begin to voice their complaints.

Roth bluntly suggested that the future of Van Halen was no longer about four music-obsessed kids getting together to make noise and party hard; more than just a band, Van Halen was now a brand, a business, in a contemporaneous interview with writer David Gans for Record magazine.

We intend to continue recording rock music with our rock band for a very long time, he said. The best method to achieve it is to regularly and frequently create new music. Simply said, a new record needs to be made.

The seventh Van Halen album's writing sessions started out tumultuous. The chemistry had changed, according to Roth. "There were screaming and delays all the time." It had the sound of a bag of sick cats.The discussions intensified, growing louder and more caustic, with threats and hands balling into fists.

It's unclear exactly what transpired after that. Eddie responded that Roth had little interest in hearing the new music he was writing, despite Roth's claims that it was dismal and depressing. According to Roth, the Van Halen brothers planned to curtail the group's tour schedule and promote their next record with just a few stadium appearances. Eddie retorted, "He was the one who proposed not doing a record and just making money on the summer circuit. Eddie denied saying this, but he said he was taking a bird's-eye view of the entire process and figured a year would fly by between writing, recording, and mixing, plus discussions about artwork, merchandise, and tour scheduling. Roth claimed Eddie told him the album would take a year to make. The guitarist yelled, "[He] put it in the press like I just wanted to rot in the studio for a year." Eddie and Alex dismissed Noel Monk as Van Halen's manager in April against Roth's desires. Eddie would subsequently assert that Roth was using Monk as his "goddamn puppet."

The rapidly deteriorating situation was made more difficult when Roth, encouraged by positive feedback for his direction of the "California Girls" music video, wrote the screenplay for the movie Crazy from the Heat, which centers on the rock star Dave, and actively started looking for funding to make the movie. In his book of the same name, the singer described the scenario of Crazy from the Heat, a "musical with a very left-of-center plot," with gravity akin to Francis Ford Coppola. Regardless of how it may have sounded in his head, reading the synopsis on paper is incredibly painful. In general, the plot would center on a cunning plan by Dave's dishonest managers to defraud the rock star of his earnings. This scheme could only be carried out once Dave had been sent off on a post-tour vacation to the imaginary "Dongo Islands," which were described as "your worst Third World," where the unfortunate innocent and his friends would stumble into "cannibal country" and suffer a fate worse than death.

A Japanese criminal cartel that is funding unethical and extremely illegal experiments aimed at isolating brain serum that, when synthesized, would give geeky white people the gift of rhythm, would somehow learn of Dave's new handlers' wicked plot and seek to warn him of their villainy. However, they would instead come across the Japanese cartel. When the conspirators realized there was "some problem with crossing the races" and decided that the only ideal test subject would be a white man with rhythm, Dave would get involved in this depraved scheme. "And they have no one else to think of but Dave."

Surprisingly, someone at CBS Pictures loved the concept and offered $10 million to support the film's production. This is evidence of the power of both Roth's public image in 1985 and the quantity of cocaine the Medelln Cartel was bringing into Los Angeles in the middle of the 1980s. The studio's support made Roth feel justified, and he duly informed the Van Halen brothers that he would be taking a break from the group.

Eddie recounted Roth telling him in a confrontation at his Pasadena estate, "I can't work with you guys anymore." "Perhaps we can get back together when I'm done with my movie," she said.
The guitarist retorted, "I ain't waiting on your ass!" "Goodbye and good luck,"

***

A blast of the guitarist's signature "shredding" appeared in a crucial scene in the time-traveling sci-fi movie Back to the Future on July 3, 1985. Marty McFly, played by Michael J. Fox, slips a cassette marked "Edward Van Halen" into a Walkman and wakes his sleeping father with a loud alarm call. This led some Van Halen fans to believe they were hearing a preview of the band's upcoming seventh album. However, when Rolling Stone published on July 4, the day of the American Independence, that "Van Halen is on permanent hold," nerdy arguments over whether or not this "bunch of noise," as Eddie called it, was or wasn't a new Van Halen song were almost immediately eclipsed.

The shocking news stated that Eddie, who is rumored to be looking for a new lead singer, is writing songs with Patty Smyth and intends to work with Pete Townsend. David Lee Roth is now working on his own film and plans to pursue acting full-time.

It took a while for the news to receive official confirmation. However, Eddie went against the grain in August and told Rolling Stone, "The band as you know it is over."The guitarist said, "Dave left to become a movie star. Even more audaciously, he asked me to write the score for him. A fresh lead singer is what I'm seeking for. 'Eddie commented, "It's strange that it's over. "I put up with his bullshit for twelve years of my life."

When word of the breakup spread, Ted Templeman was working on Aerosmith's 'comeback' record Done with Mirrors. The producer believed that the argument would end swiftly. Van Halen were ready to take Roth's place before information of the singer's identity reached him.

Eddie's immediate reaction was to re-enter the spotlight with an all-star "various artists" compilation CD, with the likes of Joe Cocker, Phil Collins, and Journey's Steve Perry singing his songs, as worried musician pals rallied around him in the wake of Roth's departure. Alex Van Halen dissuaded his younger brother Eddie from going on with the plan and advised him to look for a talented vocalist who could bring harmony and balance back into their musical family. The idea of working with Pete Townshend was also dropped, primarily because the guitarist for the Who wanted to work in London and Eddie didn't want to leave Alex and Michael Anthony out of the project. Less romantically, however, Eddie lost Townshend's personal phone number. Eddie started concentrating his efforts on persuading a family member to join the cause instead.

Patty Smyth was initially brought to her husband's attention by Valerie Bertinelli. The actress had developed a slight obsession with the New York rock band Scandal's 1984 single "The Warrior," so when she learned that the group would be opening for John Waite at the Hollywood Palladium on November 7 of the same year, she requested Eddie to take her. One step further, the guitarist joined Scandal onstage for their covers of "River Deep, Mountain High" by Ike and Tina Turner and "Maybe We Went Too Far" by Scandal. He then led Valerie backstage to meet Patty Smyth, the show's vocalist. The chemistry between the three of them was so strong that the following week Eddie and Valerie traveled to Texas to see Scandal perform at two gigs there, and the guitarist once more joined the New Yorkers on stage for their encores. Later, Smyth would pay the couple multiple visits in Los Angeles, staying the night even when Valerie was filming out of town. Eddie asked Smyth if she would consider auditioning for his band when Roth left, but timing wasn't great because the vocalist was pregnant at the time and married to New York punk pioneer Richard Hell. Eddie continued to woo Smyth even after Warners advised him to put his band on hold and focus on a solo album, saying, "If they think I'm going to experiment and futz around, doing a solo project as opposed to what I really want - just to wait and see if Roth comes back - they're off their nut." On July 27, 1985, he invited the singer, who was eight months pregnant at the time, to join him and Valerie, Late Night with David Letterman band

'"Look, I gotta know," he said. You must tell me right away. Smyth remembered. 'I responded, "I can't." He definitely wanted me to carry out the task. Over the course of a year, he repeatedly questioned me. But when he truly needed the response, I simply wasn't prepared to relocate my entire life to California. That wasn't something I expected to happen to me soon. I would have rather if he had simply said, "Hey, let's just do a record, we can call it whatever." But the manner he asked implied that I had to relocate to California, and I simply wasn't in the appropriate hormonal frame of mind for that.

That was a very ballsy idea, especially for rock 'n' roll, which is so misogynistic, according to Eddie, who was brave and witty. He just remarked, "You're a badass. You are capable. "I know I can do it, but I'm eight months pregnant!" I exclaim.

I believe we would have destroyed it. I believe that the fans and everyone else would have reacted positively because they loved and trusted Eddie and believed that he knew what he was doing. Sure, there might have been some skepticism in the media or elsewhere, but I believe we would have disproved it all.

***

In the end, and perhaps rather aptly, Van Halen's second act would start at a shop selling luxury automobiles. Former Ferrari test driver Claudio Zampolli, who is based in Van Nuys, has amassed a prestigious clientele and reputation as a seller of imported luxury cars and the go-to technician for the dim-witted Valley millionaires who collect them like baseball cards. Eddie was asking Zampolli to inspect his Lamborghini Countach when he noticed a Ferrari 512 in the shop.

Nice automobile, he remarked. Whose vehicle is that?
Zampolli answered, "Sammy Hagar's." "You should give him a call and recruit him to the band."
Eddie questioned, "You got his number?"
Hagar, who was recuperating at home after postponing a summer tour of Japan in promotion of the Ted Templeman-produced album VOA, was ready for the call.

He says, "I was working on another record with Ted Templeman and he was telling me about all the bad blood in Van Halen." He would be saying things like, "Oh, boy, those guys, man, they've got a lot of problems." I also assumed that I would receive a call when Ted said, "I think Roth is going to leave the band."

Who can they get, I mean, this is one of the biggest rock bands in the world. Because Roth was such a famous character, they can't just pick any child off the street. I reasoned, "Well, there's Ronnie James

Dio, there's Ozzy Osbourne, and there's Sammy Hagar, and that's about it." Ozzy was a wreck at the time, Dio was a member of Van Halen, and I was performing twice a week in practically every American venue. So I simply said, "They need to call me." I'm not claiming to be psychic, but I do have gut sensations and have my entire life.

Hagar, like David Lee Roth, wasn't a man who constantly doubted himself or lacked self-confidence. Hagar, who was born in Salinas, California, on October 13, 1947, was only fourteen when he made his band debut, fronting the Fabulous Castilles, and only twenty-five when he knocked on Ronnie Montrose's door in Sausalito to ask the former Van Morrison/Herbie Hancock guitarist if he'd like to start a band.

Hagar claims, "I never lacked confidence." Once I established a band and began playing in front of audiences, I realized that this is what I was meant to do and that I was good at it. I never lacked confidence, but I wasn't haughty either. I used to be a young person who would have done anything to achieve fame and money. The Edgar Winter Group, who had one of the biggest albums in the country at the time (They Only Come Out at Night) the night before, was opening for Ronnie at a sold-out Winterland, so to me Ronnie was a big rock star and my ticket to the big time. I genuinely believed I could succeed.

Montrose made the decision to listen to Hagar after being struck by her self-assurance and bravado. The two quickly accumulated an album's worth of songs and decided to start a new band.

"Ronnie and I had great chemistry at first," claims Hagar. We have twenty minutes to write a song. He wasn't a songwriter; all he had was one riff for "Rock the Nation." I, however, had a number of songs, including "Make It Last," "I Don't Want It," "One Thing on My Mind," and "Bad Motor Scooter." I also showed him the lyrics of "Space Station #5", and the two of us immediately wrote that song.

Soon after, Ted Templeman received a call from Ronnie Montrose asking if they could set up a meeting to discuss the formation of a new band. Templeman enjoyed the San Francisco guitarist, enjoyed working with Montrose on Van Morrison's Tupelo Honey record, and was reminded of Cream when he listened to Montrose's demo. He had the band set up by the summer of 1973 to record their debut album for Warners at the Sunset Sound and Amigo studios. According to Templeman, who peaked at number 133 on the Billboard 200, Montrose's failure to connect with American rock fans left him "flabbergasted." Hagar maintained his positive attitude while touring with bands like Black Oak Arkansas, Foghat, and Humble Pie. He says, "I would have loved to have had overnight success, but the prospect of hard work didn't bother me, because with my poor, blue-collar working-class background, I only knew how to do things the hard way," and that news that the album was steadily selling in Europe gave him hope. The vocalist was certain that the quartet's big break was just around the corner as they embarked on their first-ever European tour in promotion of their second album, Paper Money, released in 1974.

He recalls that after a performance in Belgium, a major publication wrote about us and featured my picture. Getting that kind of attention makes you feel special, so I was extremely delighted because I wanted to feel exceptional. But the fact that I was the subject of the review freaked Ronnie out. It was too much for his ego.

Days later, Montrose informed his singer that the band was disbanding, just in time for two sold-out performances at the Olympia in Paris.

According to Hagar, "I felt like I had been punched in the gut." "I knew something was going to happen because Ronnie was growing increasingly distant, but it was devastating." I was extremely let down. I was completely baffled by it because it was both unexpected and completely incorrect. It really irked me. It was a fairly precarious period for me because I had no money in the bank and a wife and infant at home. Ronnie might be a waste of time.

That band never advanced past the sophomore year and never graduated; the music you heard from us was immature and had only begun to emerge from the egg. We could have created some fantastic songs and developed into a truly fantastic band if we had managed to stay together and mature as a group. But Ronnie made a different choice.

Templeman, who was equally shocked by the band's breakup, gave Hagar the money to record a demo tape for Warners but decided against signing the vocalist as a solo artist.

It was first discouraging because Ted was highly influential at Warners and all of his proposals received attention, claims Hagar. But looking back, it turned out to be a blessing in disguise because I had to start over from scratch by myself. I made mistakes because I was young and innocent, but it also started me on my own path.

I believe that when I've got a little bit of "I'll show you sons of bitches!" in my head, I work the hardest and produce the best outcomes. That's beneficial for any exceptional athlete or artist, in my opinion. Being a bit rate is healthy. You require some sort of fire.

The 'Red Rocker' was in high gear by the time Templeman and Hagar collaborated once again on 1984's VOA. John Kalodner, a rising star in A&R, got Hagar signed to Geffen Records. His debut album for the company, Standing Hampton, went platinum, and the lead single from 1983's Three Lock Box, "Your Love Is Driving Me Crazy," reached the Top 20. The first single from VOA, "I Can't Drive 55," peaked at number 26 on the charts and helped its parent album surpass the one million sales mark within the year. The song's classic music video shows the singer's Ferrari 512 being chased by the California Highway Patrol. Which was around the time Claudio Zampolli's repair company received a phone call from Eddie Van Halen. Hagar consented to a meeting primarily out of curiosity.

"Wow, this may be something," he exclaimed." Steven Rosen remembers Eddie. He wanted to first meet us and assess our condition by coming down. Because he had heard some terrifying tales about my being a space case, somewhere out in the universe. Along with him was his manager, Ed Lefler. We didn't only wish to work on a project with you, we said. We want you to be a band member for life."

I remember asking myself, "What am I going to do now?" at the time. Hagar remembers. "At that time, I was seeking motivation to continue living. I had come from a very humble upbringing and had worked extremely hard my entire life. I had always been driven by fame and riches, and at that point I had plenty of both thanks to my four platinum albums in a row and my ability to sell out double arenas in nearly every American city. I was saying to myself, "I don't need any more money, and I don't need any more fame." I was incredibly wealthy, dining at the best establishments, dressing to kill, and drove Ferraris. My music was suffering from my growing sophistication, which was bad.

Unaware that the biggest hard-rock album of the previous 12 months had been written and recorded in a space that resembled "the worst bar on the planet," Hagar arrived at Van Halen's 5150 studio wearing a freshly pressed Armani suit.

He recalls with a chuckle that "these guys had cigarette butts and empty beer cans and whisky bottles everywhere, and multi-thousand dollar guitars lying upside down on the ground." The smoke made it smell terrible. Eddie emerges from the bedroom wearing sunglasses, hole-ridden clothes, drinking beer, and smoking a cigarette. Alex was still intoxicated. Not even Mike had been at home. They had stayed up all night long to wait for me. When I turn to look at myself in a suit after looking at these people, I think, "I look like a fucking idiot." This group truly embodies rock 'n' roll.

When Black Sabbath played Summerfest at Anaheim Stadium on September 23, 1978, Roth, Anthony, and the Van Halen brothers pretended to parachute into the stadium, and Hagar shared an afternoon stage with the band, Hagar first got to know the Van Halen members. Eddie revealed to Hagar backstage that the group used to play Montrose songs in clubs. From Hagar's perspective, the guitarist struck him as "one of the nicest, sweetest, and humblest rock stars on the planet."

He claims, "From the outside, I was impressed by Van Halen." "I liked them because they wrote hard-rock pop songs," I said. Eddie played the guitar with such musicality and, because he favored major chords, it had a really distinctive, cool, and edgy yet beautiful sound. It felt simultaneously weighty and nearly feeble. In the same way that [Led Zeppelin drummer] John Bonham always made Jimmy Page sound heavy, so Alex always made Eddie's playing hard, even when he was playing cutie-pie riffs, the band's sound was made heavy by Ted Templeman and Donn Landee's production. Roth's antics didn't appeal to me. He didn't seem to appeal to any guys, but I think they did. Like Howard Stern famously stated, "If David's biggest fans ran into him in a bar, they'd kick his ass!"

The two vocalists were smitten with one another. When Roth asked aloud to a writer at the start of the decade, "quite what manner of a man was Sam, writing songs only about cars and not women," Hagar replied, calling Roth a "faggot" and implying that the leader of Van Halen sought a "relationship" with him. (In response, Roth said in 1982, "Sammy obviously has a social problem. I believe it is due to a lack of education.
Eddie later told Steven Rosen that "Dave always hated Sammy." "I've never known why." Dave would constantly belittle him, saying, "That little mother has nothing on me." Where is that even coming from, I would ponder. Why the hostility?

But I'll always remember the first tune Sammy and I jammed on. "Summer Nights" was playing. The tape was being played by Donn Landee. We replayed it and were like, "Holy sh*t. Our entire lives, where have you been?

Hagar remembers, "We just cranked up." 'I just start skating and singing after they had already composed some of the ideas for the tunes to "Summer Nights" and "Good Enough." Because I recently got the majority of my hair shaved off, leaving only a small amount of poodle poof on top, Alex is making fun of my haircut. And I'm saying, "Fuck you guys, let's go outside," in jest. All day long, we recorded what we did on cassettes. It was so rock 'n' roll when I played one of these tapes when I arrived home at two in the morning. "Fucking wow!" I exclaimed. It just sounded incredibly new when I heard how musical Ed and Alex were and how Michael could sing over me. Wow, this is like Cream, I thought. I thought, "This is wonderful, this is fucking good, this is better than what I can do on

my own." It was very subtle and lyrical. Eddie Van Halen provided the motivation I was looking for.'
To Ed Lefler, Hagar replied, "I'm doing it."

Despite the positive sentiments between the parties and their shared desire to explore what could result from combining their abilities, there remained the little but important issue of Hagar being under contract to Geffen Records. When Mo Ostin called to inquire about the possibility of Sammy Hagar joining Van Halen and the Warners stable, David Geffen, an observant and shrewd businessman, realized that he held the whip hand and handled their negotiations accordingly. According to Hagar, Geffen agreed to lend Warners their most valuable asset for the duration of one record, after which they demanded the rights to a brand-new Hagar solo album. On that solo album, David Geffen requested a 100% cut of the label revenues, and on Hagar's debut Van Halen album, he requested a 50% cut. When the horse trading was finally resolved to everyone's satisfaction, Ostin would remark to Hagar, "Sammy, you have no fucking idea what you cost me."

Ostin agreed to go see the freshly formed foursome perform some brand-new music at 5150 in the fall of 1985. One can only picture the scowl on the seasoned music mogul's face as he entered the filthy studio and discovered the best guitarist of his generation sitting behind a keyboard after having staked the farm on hard rock's newest supergroup. The upbeat, keyboard-driven song "Why Can't This Be Love" was the first tune the quartet decided to play on broadcast. The four musicians waited for Ostin's response as the song came to a finish.
Ostin said, "I smell money," grinning as he licked his finger and held it in the air.

The first Farm Aid concert, a huge fundraising event organized by Willie Nelson, John Mellencamp, and Neil Young to aid American farmers facing financial ruin, was held at the Memorial Stadium in Champaign, Illinois, on September 22. During Hagar's set, Hagar revealed the creative partnership between Van Halen and their new frontman. Hagar, Foreigner, and Bon Jovi were the only hard-rock acts scheduled on an incredible bill that also included Bob Dylan,

Tom Petty and the Heartbreakers, Johnny Cash, John Fogerty, Roy Orbison, Joni Mitchell, Billy Joel, and more, but Hagar had a trick up his sleeve with Eddie waiting in the wings to join his band for a set-closing cover of Led Zeppelin's "Rock and Roll." After Hagar introduced "I Can't Drive 55" as "a song for all you tractor-pulling motherfuckers," the live feed of the band's performance was abruptly pulled from the TV and radio coverage, meaning only the more attentive spectators in the stadium would hear his good news. This slightly diminished the impact of the big reveal. However, "Van Hagar" had been freed.

The newly reformed band needed a new producer because Ted Templeman was already committed to working on David Lee Roth's solo record. Mick Jones, the guitarist for Foreigner, enters at Hagar's suggestion and issues a warning to prepare for the unexpected.
Sammy reportedly responded to Jones, "Mick, you and I have been around awhile," but let me tell you, this is something else. Hold on tight and take in the scenery!"

Van Halen chose to play one of their stronger collaborations, the full-tilt, metallic 'Get Up', as an introductory song for the well-mannered, polite English guitarist.

Jones informed them, "I've never heard anything like that in my life." It sounds like four men are fighting and beating the crap out of one another inside the speaker cabinets. I'm in.'
Van Halen fans across the world questioned what kind of future the band may have without its talismanic former lead singer as the quintet prepared to work with Jones at 5150. David Lee Roth joined in as well, unable to hold back.

Without David Lee Roth, he wondered if there was still a Van Halen. But I'm aware that without David Lee Roth, nobody is interested in Van Halen.

Eddie Van Halen called Roth a "clown" and gave a scathing reply. He said, "The issue with Roth was that he forgot who wrote the songs." I composed them. The songs themselves represent the soul of our music. I never gave his words any attention. It didn't matter a whit to me what he was singing about.

Roth said, "I'm sure that Edward will play every bit as well as he ever has." "I never claimed he was anything other than an excellent guitarist. He's merely an unremarkable person.

Chapter 5: Feels Wonderful

Ed Lefler struggled to suppress a smirk as Sammy Hagar, Michael Anthony, Eddie, and Alex Van Halen entered his suite at the Ritz-Carlton hotel in Atlanta and slouched down one by one. The four musicians were still getting the hang of their tour three weeks into a run of live performances that was expected to last from late March to early November. They were still honing the daily rituals and routines that would help to reduce anxiety or at least distort reality in the hours between hotel check-ins and gig stage times before the familiar adrenaline surges kicked in and all manners were abandoned once more. Nobody had anticipated hastily scheduled early-afternoon band meetings with management.

A little too long was spent by Lefler gazing silently at his gruff charges before Hagar lost her cool.
Ed, what the fuck?
A vintage champagne bottle was taken out of one of the silver ice buckets that Lefler had sent up to his suite by reaching behind his chair.
"Billboard No. One."

***

'Why Can't This Be Love,' the first song the band performed for Mo Ostin at Eddie's studio, was published four weeks prior to Van Halen's 5150 album's official release date on March 24, 1986. The most famous and tautological line of the song was uttered by Hagar, who wondered that only time would tell if they would stand the test of time. The song's first-week sales were a strong start, guaranteeing Top 10 debuts in the US, UK, Germany, and Australia.
The foursome spent November 1985 through February 1986 working on 5150. Making the album was "a breeze" for Eddie. The guitarist was especially effusive in his praise for the new frontman of his band. He said to Steven Rosen, "I don't know if I could have gotten out of Dave what I can get out of Sammy. I'm not sure if this is disparaging Dave, but Sammy is simply a superior singer and can carry out any task I give him.He has altered my life. Seriously.'

Eddie had been held back, in my opinion, by Roth's vocal limitations, claims Hagar. Songs like "Dreams" had been sitting on tape for a year or two when Ted Templeman would have objected, saying, "No, Dave can't sing that." Eddie was therefore playing cassettes as I got in, and I would say, "Wow, fuck, yeah, let's go!" Van Halen was able to elevate their performance. Eddie's dissatisfaction with the previous band, in my opinion, would have led to its dissolution. I believed I was the savior because of the impression he gave me. We bonded in a wonderful way.

When he heard me sing, Ed freaked out, and Michael Anthony and Al did too. "Holy shit," they were saying, "this guy has rhythm in his voice, he has pitch and a range from hell." "Hey, Eddie, how about a groove like this?" I may ask while picking up a guitar. He would say, "Holy sh*t, let me play organ," after hearing you play some rhythm. We were dispersed everywhere. It was such a mutual source of inspiration that it began to improve both of our musical skills. Everyone nearby experienced chills. It was enchanted.

Being organized, composed, patient, and motivating, Mick Jones also contributed in the studio by cutting the fat from the original demo of "Why Can't This Be Love" to highlight its melodic hooks and co-writing and rearranging "Dreams," which enabled Hagar to give a career-best vocal performance.

Jones added, "I was able to push Sammy to new heights." 'Literally. He was hyperventilating as a result of his high-pitched singing. Nearly lost consciousness.
The frontman of Foreigner adopted a different approach with Eddie, as he explained to Classic Rock writer Paul Elliott, sensibly letting the guitarist do his thing in light of his tendency to rebel when confronted by authoritative figures.

There wasn't much Jones could have done to enhance Eddie's performances. He wasn't under the influence of drugs; rather, when he played, he simply entered a trance state.

In these circumstances, Jones was reminded of his interactions with Jimi Hendrix in the late 1960s, when the American guitarist was the opening act on a European tour and Jones was the guitarist for French rock 'n' roll icon Johnny Hallyday.

When I played with Eddie, it was the first time I'd encountered a guitarist with a comparable talent, said Jones, "who had that thing running through him from up above."
He was a lovely man all around and very modest. No pretense, attitude, or airs. I found working with him to be hypnotic.
Jones told Rolling Stone, "We had a good time" After the training, we used to race vehicles in a variety of expensive sports and along Mulholland. The Lamborghini he owned. Sammy may have owned a red Ferrari. And I had a reliable vintage American automobile. I spanked him multiple times!"

The only serious hiccup during the process was when Donn Landee had what Jones kindly referred to as "a bad moment," which was reminiscent of the darker times in the making of 1984
.

Jones said, "He locked himself in the studio and threatened to burn the tapes." It felt like one of those scenarios where someone was going to commit suicide since there was a standoff for about a day. He was really sensitive. But ultimately, we managed to calm him down.

The quartet started pre-release promotional responsibilities with local, national, and worldwide media outlets at 5150 after the record was securely in the can and out of Landee's hands. One of those called to Eddie's studio complex for an audience with the new-look quartet was English music critic Sylvie Simmons, a longtime fan who had originally interviewed the band when they backed Black Sabbath in 1978. Naturally, the former frontman of the band came up in conversation. At first, Eddie and Alex were diplomatic, politely answering the journalist's questions while continually bringing up the band's optimism in the present. But eventually, Alex had had enough of skirting the issue.

He remarked, "I imagine you're going to print this anyhow, so I'm going to say it: basically, Roth's world was his world when he was around. Everyone avoided breathing incorrectly while that character was present.

"Not scared..." Eddie chimed in.

'Horseshit!' Alex stated coldly. "Man, it was the truth. He taught us all how to walk and talk, as well as how to dress. He wouldn't permit anyone to speak out of turn.

Eddie finally said, "The guy is an asshole."

***

5150's slick, polished professionalism was never going to be appealing to everyone. Longtime viewers bemoaned its lack of spontaneity, lack of humor, and lack of any sense of real danger, foolishness, or adventure. The adults had taken control, for better or worse. 'I know there are people who are like, 'Oh, I liked early Van Halen better, Sammy wrecked it," Hagar said, going on the defense for once. 'But this was the music that Eddie delivered to me. Although I wrote the words and melodies, Eddie wanted to make this music, and I felt vindicated by the album's sales numbers. Whitney Houston's self-titled debut album was knocked off the top of the Billboard 200 in its third week of sales after 5150, which didn't use a single promotional video, sold a million copies in just two weeks. With just three words, Hagar encapsulated the band's emotions: "We felt invincible."

The domestic tragedy, however, was hidden under the public victory. Eddie was overjoyed when Valerie found out she was pregnant in January 1986. She went to the doctor in March after enduring excruciating discomfort, and he told her that she had miscarried. In an effort to ease her suffering, Valerie persuaded herself that the miscarriage was God's retribution for a one-night stand she had the year prior, when she was depressed at her husband's lack of attention and at her lowest point.

There was more pain to come. Eddie and Alex got phone calls from their mother on May 24, just before a second sold-out Van Halen performance at the Alpine Valley Music Theatre in East Troy, Wisconsin, letting them know that their father Jan had suffered a serious heart attack. Valerie, the brothers, and a private jet were leased to take them back to California, and the group arrived at the medical facility where Jan was receiving treatment. Jan, who was always cheery, made an effort to downplay his situation by assuring his sons that he would soon be released from the hospital and be back on his feet. Maintaining a constant presence by Jan's bedside was not an option for his sons because Van Halen was committed to arena shows through 3 November. However, over the course of the following five months, the brothers racked up tens of thousands of air miles as they took advantage of every opportunity in the tour schedule to fly back home to check on their father's progress. But Jan went away on December 9 at the age of 66, surrounded by his wife Eugenia and his two sons.

Eddie's youngest son was especially hard-hit by Jan's passing, and his cocaine and alcohol use skyrocketed. The musician barricaded himself in his studio for days at a time to self-medicate.
Every day, according to Valerie Bertinelli, "seemed to become more and more of a battle, whether we were fighting each other, or just fighting the sadness of life," as she noted in her autobiography.
In a brave and open-hearted interview with the women's magazine Redbook, Bertinelli discussed the problems the marriage was having; her worry for her husband was clear in every word. She said, "He doesn't hurt me, but he hurts himself."

While working on his debut solo album with Ted Templeman, guitarist Steve Vai, bassist Billy Sheehan, and drummer Gregg Bissonette, Roth had revealed his decision to leave Van Halen in a no-holds-barred interview with Creem's Dave DiMartino in June. Roth obviously felt the need to make some headlines before his album's planned July release because his previous band was the first to release new music.

The guys keep talking about how miserable they were for the previous 10, 12, and how the music was bad, but now they're going to keep talking about how fantastic everything is. Edward Van Halen, poor guy, he had to lie to himself! Surviving the barrage of Maseratis with difficulty! forced to persevere after one Lamborghini after another! Can you even begin to comprehend how anxious the poor child must be? However, he is now 30 years old and no longer a child.

Roth yelled, "You don't go bullshitting the public like that." You don't behave that way toward your supporters. Van Halen was -- and still is -- a huge part of who I am. That band had my entire heart and my entire existence; I gave my everything to them. You simply can't continue to treat the general folks like idiots when there is mindless word drool all over the pages about how it "stunk." Yes, we detested it, but Dave made us do it. Large, terrible Dave

"You know, I said a few7 things in anger for which I should apologize," That same summer, Eddie confirmed as much to David Fricke of Rolling Stone while maintaining his sincere sadness over the breakup of the original line-up.
I sobbed and felt depressed. I criticized him in the media because I was furious and wounded.
Roth remained unimpressed.

Edward now turns that impish little "Ohhh, I'm so sorry," as they realize how ugly their little hatchet job on me reads. Roth sneered. I don't believe it. Neither does the general population, in my opinion.
Roth's Eat 'Em and Smile was a terrific hard-rock debut; it was preceded by the fantastic swagger of "Yankee Rose," featuring former Frank Zappa sideman Steve Vai in sparkling form. The album peaked at number four on the Billboard 200 in late August. When it came time to tour with Eat 'Em and Smile, he encountered half-full arenas that his former bandmates had filled twice over earlier in the year. However, if he had imagined that his solo career would surpass that of his former band, he was mistaken. The singer's decision to hold a press conference in Toronto in October 1986 to protest his apparent perception that Van Halen were seeking uncompromising 'love us and hate him' allegiance from fans torn in their emotions had more than a whiff of desperation.

With his next remark directed towards Eddie, Roth affirmed, "I'll rise to the challenge." I'll eat you for breakfast, buddy, eat you and smile if we must make a comparison.

Back in California, Valerie gave Eddie a stern ultimatum: either he fire his drug dealer and swear to stop drinking, or she would leave their marriage out of fear that her grieving husband's suicidal tendencies would cause him to die young like his father had. Eddie did nothing but watch her leave, still numbed and lost in self-pity.

Valerie made the decision to conduct an intervention for her estranged husband as the new year got underway because she was unable to give up on the guy she loved. It was a hard and emotional experience for Eddie, who felt deceived, victimized, and bullied as his bandmates, family, and closest friends took turns pleading with him to get treatment for his alcohol and drug misuse problems. The guitarist consented to enter himself into the Betty Ford Clinic in Rancho Mirage, California, for treatment when his temper had calmed down and he realized that his actions were endangering everything he had lived and worked for.

Sammy Hagar argues that confronting someone is difficult. 'You can't convince someone to change their way of life unless they are willing to do so, especially if they are a wealthy and well-known rock star. If you try to influence their way of life or their routines, they'll be like, "Fuck you, you're fired!" When you're wealthy and well-known, most people won't tell you anything, so you can get away with murder since whatever you do or say will be accepted. Nobody can make those significant changes before they are prepared. Ted Templeman once told me: "No rock star getting their ass kissed is going to change anything until they hit rock bottom; it's only when they lose everything that they wake up." He is absolutely correct.

"At that time, Eddie and Al both had significant drinking issues. I saw it, but at first it didn't worry me because they could play when we approached the instruments. The fact that these people could perform well when intoxicated made me think, "Wow, there is no problem here." And even if they had stayed up all night to complete it, they would have been there if we had said, "Be at the studio tomorrow at noon." You can easily get away with becoming a rock star if you have a drug or alcohol addiction. Sorry to break it to you, but you can. Rock stars are spoiled rotten, but you can't if you work in construction and have to get up at five every morning to drive a truck.

Eddie told the Seattle Post-Intelligencer, "At first, Sammy thought9 Alex and I were drinking because we were so happy to have a singer, that we were celebrating." Then he understood that was how we behaved every day. I believe he was a little frightened.

He asserted to Billboard, "I didn't drink to party." "I treated alcohol and cocaine as personal matters." They'd be useful for my work. The combination of the blow and drink keeps you alert. If I had not been in that mental condition, I'm sure there were musical things I would not have tried.

I needed booze to function because I was an alcoholic.
After experiencing a "lost" period following the death of his father, Alex sought treatment for his alcoholism in April 1987.
I partied too much, he admitted. I had three months to kill when I got home [after the 5150 tour]. I merely went outside and fastened a large one. We don't want to see you dead, trust us, the band members had the guts to express. You ought to take action. I had gone outside.

Alcohol is humorous. Although it is a common practice at parties and is socially acceptable, it has the power to manipulate you.
Sammy Hagar enlisted Eddie as a co-producer that spring and got to work on the solo record he promised Geffen. I Never Said Goodbye, which was finished in ten days with only one guitar solo (on "Eagles Fly") by Eddie, would become Hagar's highest-charting solo album, reaching number 14 in mid-August. Van Halen went back to 5150 the next month to start writing their eighth studio album. The quartet approached the album with a newfound maturity and a sense of bursting confidence inspired by the six million domestic sales of 5150, self-producing alongside Donn Landee. Their failure may have been caused by this. It's completely understandable that there was little hunger or urgency driving the group's songwriting during the leisurely seven months they spent on OU812, having defeated Roth, silenced the doubters at Warners, and proven they didn't need their mentor Ted Templeman's guiding hands or golden ears to deliver commercial success. As he hopped between his property in Malibu and his vacation home in picturesque Cabo San Lucas, on Mexico's

Baja California Peninsula, there was little to enrage the self-possessed artist, who admittedly functioned best with a vengeful "I'll show you sons of bitches!" fire inside. Eddie insisted that the album should be called "Rock 'n' Roll" because that is exactly what it is. 'It ain't heavy metal, it's not hard rock, it's rock 'n' roll' - and he had a point, for across its nine tracks the set dabbles with raunchy blues ('Black and Blue'), Zeppelin-esque grooving ('Cabo Wabo'), classic VH power-boogie ('Source of Infection', part of the same lineage as 'I'm the One' and 'Hot for Teacher') and synth pop ('When It's Love'), without ever getting wild or threatening to upset the neighbors. The finger-picked acoustic country blues of "Finish What Ya Started," written after Eddie coaxed his Malibu neighbor Hagar out of bed at 2 in the morning with a bottle of Jack Daniel's whiskey in one hand and an acoustic guitar in the other, is the only genuinely interesting curveball on an album intended to consolidate the group's wide appeal. 'Finish What Ya Started' is marred by Hagar's creepy, middle-aged sex-pest lyrics, just like a number of other tracks on OU812 like 'Source of Infection', 'Black and Blue', and 'Sucker in a 3 Piece' - He said that it was "not my best stuff," yet it's likely the only time throughout a good but unspectacular set when Van Halen aren't in autopilot. Van Halen appeared to be settling into producing the kind of finely manicured arena rock one might expect to hear soundtracking Don Simpson/Jerry Bruckheimer Hollywood movies while Guns N' Roses were igniting Los Angeles with the explosive Appetite for Destruction. The moving dedication 'This one's for you, Pa' was inserted on the album's inside sleeve as a token of respect and thanks to the man who had shared their entire musical vision with Eddie and Alex, but, in all honesty, the album's grooves lacked much of Jan Van Halen's cheeky, rebellious spirit.

Sammy Hagar recommended to Ed Lefler that it was time for Van Halen to make the transition to headlining stadiums since he was confident the band had another multi-platinum hit album under their belt. If Mötley Crüe, who are huge Van Halen fans, were able to draw 60,000 rock fans to Bill Graham's (almost) annual Day on the Green festival in 1987 as the headliners, then surely Van Halen, "the biggest band in the world," could do the same across the country with their own custom festival package. Hagar reasoned that the fact that no one had ever tried such a massive project before would only heighten the spectacle and cement Van Halen's status as true rock legends.

Van Halen essentially wanted to write 12 pages of rock 'n' roll history, according to Louis Messina, the head promoter for PACE Concerts in Texas. Messina, the long-running and wildly popular Texxas Jam festival's promoter, was a well regarded and well-connected figure in the live music world, and it was to him that Lefler first inquired about the viability of Hagar's ambitious plan. The promoter's immediate response was positive: "I'm surprised no one has tried it before," he remarked. "It's such a natural idea." Within a few weeks, he presented Lefler with some figures, suggesting a 28-date, 23-city tour, with a potential audience of 1.7 million, to take place from the end of May to the end of July. If all tickets were sold at the suggested price of $25, the gross box office receipts would be $42 million. Messina concluded by saying that if packaged properly, it might succeed. The next task was to get a bill passed that would support the event and make it the summer's most sought-after event.

The first name on the list was a given because Van Halen and the Scorpions had a long-standing relationship. When David Lee Roth turned 24 in Hamburg during Black Sabbath's 1978 Never Say Die! tour, Rudolf Schenker and Klaus Meine of the Scorpions partied with the young Californians. Van Halen had previously covered songs from the Uli Jon Roth era, including "Speedy's Coming" and "Catch Your Train." The German quintet's tenth studio album, Savage Amusement, was scheduled to be released in April 1988. Scorpions' 1985 World Wide Live double album had sold more than a million copies in the US, so the timing was ideal. Dokken, a Los Angeles hardrock band featuring George Lynch, a former Boyz guitarist, seemed like a good choice for the middle spot on the bill because their fourth album, Back for the Attack, had been certified platinum in January 1988 and their singles, "Dream Warriors," "Burning Like a Flame," and "Prisoner," had been played on rock radio stations all over the country. Messina nominated Hamburg's Kingdom Come, a hard-rocking five-piece who recently signed with Polydor and are already drawing attention for the overt Led Zeppelin plagiarism on their self-titled first album. Metallica, an uncompromising quartet from San Francisco who were quickly outgrowing their "thrash metal" roots, was suggested by Dokken's management, Q Prime, to take over the show's vacant early afternoon slot. The group's third album, Master of Puppets, had sold a million copies worldwide without a single or video to promote it, and James Hetfield and Lars Ulrich's band had proved their mettle on arena stages as the support act on Ozzy Osbourne's Ultimate Sin Justice also for all. The combination of artists, in Messina's opinion, would appeal to a wide range of hard-rock/heavy metal fans. To tie the bill together, he suggested licensing the well-known Monsters of Rock brand name from UK promoter Maurice Jones. Bit Lefler. Van Halen members promoted the tour as the live event of the year at a multi-band press conference that kicked off the historic trek at the King Kong Encounter ride at Universal Studios in Los Angeles.

Eddie stated, "When I was younger, I would have killed to go to something like this," while Sammy Hagar hoped that every person who bought a ticket would leave the nine-hour performance exclaiming, "That was the best show I've ever seen in my life."
The way I see it, this tour is kind of like one huge sandwich, you know," Alex Van Halen said, assessing the package. Which bite—the first or the last—is the best? Who cares as long as you consume it all, anyway?

The Monsters of Rock tour offered every indication that it would be a monumental undertaking. Van Halen would have three full stage sets that would jump one another throughout the nation to accommodate the three gigs per week timetable. 971 tonnes of equipment, including a 250,000-watt sound system and an 850,000-watt lighting system to illuminate the seven-story stage, would be needed for the play, and it would all need to be hauled by 56 48-foot-long trucks. Yes, heavy metal.

The trip would be notable for Eddie Van Halen for only one reason: it would be his first sober tour.
In April 1988, as his band was getting ready for their largest tour yet, he told Rolling Stone, "I just asked the guys14 the other day if we could not have any alcohol backstage." I don't believe I have been completely sober for the past ten years of my life. I would wake up

and drink a beer before I had anything to eat. I've been making an effort to improve. Since it worked for my brother, I went to Betty Ford and the whole schtick. April will mark his first year of sobriety. I've abstained for 20 days. And I'm beginning to feel better and see the light at the end of the tunnel.

He continued, "The thing is, you can't do it for other people." 'You know, my dad passed away in December of last year from alcohol-related causes. He begged if we would stop drinking and partying, and I tried to do it for him. I made an effort to do it for my wife. I made an effort to do it for my brother. Additionally, I did no good for myself. I went on a drinking binge after leaving Betty Ford, and I ended up receiving a motorbike DUI charge.

The Monsters of Rock tour began with a three-night (May 27–29) concert at the Alpine Valley Music Theatre, Wisconsin, in front of a combined audience of 96,768 during the same week that OU812 debuted at number one on the Billboard chart. Not every performance would be as successful: in Oxford, Maine, a day of torrential rain ensured that only about a thousand hardy souls remained to watch the headliners at the Oxford Plains Speedway, and a proposed second performance at Giants Stadium in New Jersey was scrapped due to weak ticket sales, which Louis Messina called "the biggest mystery in the world." The Memorial Coliseum in Los Angeles was more hospitable, with an attendance record for the tour of 80,144 on July 24. The California trio, however, was unceremoniously upstaged by Metallica here on home soil, who stole the show.

James Hetfield and Lars Ulrich, the band's founding members, left behind a city that was essentially oblivious to their musical charms when they first moved from Los Angeles to San Francisco in February 1983. Five years later, LA's metal scene gave their prodigal sons a frenzy-inducing welcome home. While Ennio Morricone's "The Ecstasy of Gold," which served as their intro song, was still playing, their first stadium performance in the city descended into anarchy. The first to leave their assigned seats and rush to the front were those closest to the stage, but soon thousands more fans began to surge out of the stands to join them, trampling fences and overturning security guards. The band was forced to leave the stage after five songs out of concern for their safety as yellow-shirted security personnel battled to control a crowd that was now tossing safety barriers, seats, bottles, plastic glasses, and whatever else it could get its hands on.

'Nothing Van Halen accomplished [on] Sunday altered the earlier notion that Metallica is crafting the metal of the time,' LA Times reviewer Steve Hochman observed, 'and likely the future.'
Sammy Hagar had a similar reaction to the group.
He predicted that Metallica will become the new rock kings, saying, "Just wait and see."

The frontman of Van Halen was going through a bit of a confidence crisis as the band's tour in support of OU812 was coming to an end. Hagar claimed to have thought, "Maybe the honeymoon's over," after learning that his second album with the band had sold about half as many copies as 5150, still an amazing four million copies.

Eddie was feeling uninspired and was drinking a lot once more. The guitarist who had contributed so much to defining the sound of the 1980s would experience an unfortunate conclusion to the decade on its final night. Eddie was spending New Year's Eve in Malibu with his wife's family, but as he drank more Jägermeister, his mood grew gloomier, and he made the decision to leave the party before the clock struck midnight. In an effort to conceal her husband's car keys after realizing he was not competent to drive, Valerie and her husband got into a fight. Eddie became more hostile when Valerie's father attempted to step in. He finally stopped being belligerent when his father-in-law delivered a tender right hand to the side of his face, cracking a cheekbone.

Valerie drove her confused husband to the closest medical facility, where the events that caused his injuries were discussed. Although the injuries to Eddie's face would heal, the doctor who was inspecting him said, "You might want to check yourself in someplace and get help."

The guitarist would return to treatment for the first twenty-eight days of the new decade, ready to listen to someone in authority for once.

Chapter 6: Distance

One puzzled local approached a uniformed sergeant as NYPD patrolmen patiently shooed rubbernecking tourists away from the MacDougal Street entrance to Café Wha?
So, the real Van Halen is performing here tonight, right?

On January 5, 2012, Interscope Records sent invitations to a Van Halen press conference being held at Manny Roth's legendary Greenwich Village club. At the time, it was assumed that the press conference was being held to officially announce the release of a new Van Halen studio album, the band's first for Jimmy Iovine's label and their first with David Lee Roth since 1984. The rush to acquire guest-list spots when it was discovered that the Californian foursome would actually be playing at the tiny, 250-seat subterranean venue was positively unsightly. By the time the show started, Cafe Wha? was as crowded as a Katz's Deli pastrami sandwich.

In his introduction, David Lee Roth remarked, "It's like getting into a rocket in here, and it's a rocket that comes from way, way back in our past all the way into what the future is going to look like." "Ladies and gentlemen, welcome to Occupy Van Halen."

If the 2012 iteration of "Diamond" Dave lacked a little bit of Hollywood glitz, his shark-like smile and carnival barker pattern more than made up for it. He wore brown Carhartt overalls and a newsboy cap.

With a wink to his Uncle Manny, the singer jived, "It took us fifty years to get this gig." "Entry into the Rock and Roll Hall of Fame was simpler."
A total of zero songs representing Van Halen's second and third acts, featuring Sammy Hagar and Gary Cherone, could be seen by those who were close enough to the stage to read the thirteen song titles printed in black writing on the set lists posted to the amplifiers and stage. Even more unexpectedly for an album-launch showcase, there didn't seem to be any new songs listed, with 'She's the Woman' being

the only one that wouldn't be recognized by anyone who had even a passing familiarity with the six Roth-era studio albums, which date back to the quartet's club days. But later, when they weren't pressed up against America's largest hard-rock band playing a set of jukebox standards at ear-splitting volume, they would have time to reflect on the significance of this.

I told you we were returning, Roth mumbled. Tell us you missed us! Say it with sincerity!
When reviewing the concert for the New York Times, the academic Jon Pareles observed that Van Halen "is still one of the most limber bands in hard rock, with a higher center of gravity than most." "Eddie Van Halen's guitar is in constant, multi-personality dialogue with itself," according to one critic. It will riff power chords and then respond with leads that writhe from the whammy bar, scamper in notes tapped on the fingerboard, or screech from a scrape up a string. The songs were still testaments to overactive teenage hormones and musicians who recall them as the band sock its riffs and Eddie Van Halen filigreed them with virtuoso guitar.

For the record, Van Halen is still fantastic. For Grantland, heavy metal memoir author Chuck Klosterman, author of the incredibly amusing Fargo Rock City, wrote. They were totally, utterly, wholly fantastic... Eddie Van Halen's guitar playing can be compared to seeing a nuclear bomb explode from the warhead up.

* At least informally, David Lee Roth returned to Van Halen as early as spring 2000. The reunion of rock's most volublest frontman and its most talented guitarist, which had been a marriage of convenience in 1973, appeared necessary after Van Halen III. In what appeared like a none-too-subtle ground-razing exercise ahead of relaunching the group, Warners reissued remastered editions of the six Roth-era albums only, and when Spin selected a Neil Zlozower photo of a decidedly underdressed Roth circa 1980 for the cover image of its October 2000 'The 100 Sleaziest Moments in Rock' issue, the timing seemed right for California's hard-raunch kings to strut back into the spotlight. Even though the band agreed to record three brand-new songs Roth thought were "astonishing," commercial disputes slowed things down. Eddie quickly had more important things on his mind.

When the guitarist's tongue's abnormal scar tissue was discovered during a routine dental examination in January 2000, he was directed to a specialist at UCLA Medical Center. After a portion of his tongue was cut off and biopsied, the results showed that the lump was malignant. Eddie hypothesized that the brass and copper guitar picks he was chewing on might have carried the electromagnetic radiation emitted at 5150; however, his medical professionals argued that chain smoking nonstop since he was twelve may have had a greater impact on his poor health. Eddie vowed to resign to the physicians and his grieving wife. After approximately a month, his willpower gave out.

Fans of Van Halen who visited the band's official website on April 26 were greeted by a greeting from the guitarist.

I apologize for taking so long to personally address this matter. But dealing with cancer can be a very particular and private thing. I believe it is now appropriate to update you on my location. Just before spring break, I underwent an examination at Cedars-Sinai with three oncologists and three head and neck surgeons, and I was informed that I am cancer-free and healthier than ever. There's a good likelihood that I'll be cancer-free soon, though it's difficult to predict when. I just want to express my gratitude to you all for your support and concern.

The musician wouldn't post again for another thirteen months, notifying followers on May 9, 2002, that he had received a "100% clean bill of health, from head to toe." Eddie concluded his letter by thanking everyone for their "well thoughts and prayers" and adding, "Now it's time to really go back to the music and the joy... Party away, and we'll get in touch with you soon.

People magazine announced Eddie and Valerie's separation the following month.

In Losing It, Valerie stated, "After 20 years, I was done making excuses for Ed and his reliance on drugs and alcohol." I had had enough of endangering my own life. I had been promising myself for twenty years that he would get well. If that weren't the case, I would have been muttering, "Poor guy, he's got such a big heart, but look at how much pain he's in." I could find justifications for everything. But the well had dried up.

Warners also made the decision to terminate their record deal with Van Halen, bringing an end to their 23-year collaboration with the group. One can only imagine how Eddie felt when, in April, David Lee Roth and Sammy Hagar announced a twenty-one-date summer co-headlining tour, which Hagar later acknowledged was at least partially driven by a desire to "piss off Van Halen and get the fans worked up." This was a time of intense personal and professional change for Eddie. The tour was first billed as "Song for Song, the Heavyweight Champs of Rock and Roll," but soon after its debut, fans wryly dubbed it "The Sans Halen Tour." It was entirely expected that it would result in turmoil, with cancelled concerts, acrimonious mudslinging from both sides, and a trampling of Van Halen's reputation.

Eddie didn't really require any help in this area at this difficult period. For reasons that are completely beyond comprehension, the guitarist arranged a jam session with jock-metal icons Limp Bizkit in 2003. At the time, the band had lost innovative guitarist Wes Borland and their third album, Chocolate Starfish and the Hot Dog Flavored Water, had passed the six million mark in American sales. In response to an Interscope Records executive's suggestion that Eddie and Limp Bizkit frontman Fred Durst collaborate, Durst at least had the decency to dismiss the notion, adding, "That would be hilarious." The worst band ever jams with the finest guitarist ever. Eddie, however, emphasized the concept more than was necessary. He allegedly told Durst, "Fuck it, let's jam."

The event, which was held in a home in the Hollywood Hills where Limp Bizkit were holding auditions, did not go well. Eddie is said to have stormed out after his new friends refused to stop smoking marijuana in his presence. The next day, Eddie phoned Durst to request that his equipment be returned to 5150, but when the singer didn't respond for twenty-four hours, the guitarist decided to act as his own repo man. The subsequent events are described in the photo book Eruption in the Canyon: 212 Days & Nights with the Genius of Eddie Van Halen by photographer and cameraman Andrew Bennett.

According to Bennett, Eddie once purchased an assault vehicle from a military auction. It is illegal and has a shiny gun mount on the rear. Eddie drove the assault vehicle across Beverly Hills and then parked it in the front yard of the residence where Limp Bizkit was practicing. He exited without a shirt on, with his hair pulled back into a Samurai bun on top of his head, his jeans held up by a piece of rope, and his combat boots taped shut. And he was holding a pistol.

Then Bennett recalled Eddie saying, "That asshole answered the door," to him. "Where's my shit, motherfucker?" I said as I put my gun to that stupid fucking red hat of his. That stupid idiot just yelled at one of his workers to grab my shit as he turned to face him.

***

Sammy Hagar invited Alex Van Halen and his family to ring in the New Year with him and his family at their Laguna Beach home on December 31, 2003, and the Van Halens accepted. Before the clock struck twelve, Alex's phone rang. He handed it to Hagar, who recognized the voice on the other end as being that of an upset and worn-out Eddie.
The guitarist said, "Why did you leave the band?"

Hagar was speechless for once.
Warners had an idea for a second Van Halen greatest hits collection at the beginning of 2004. It would be called The Best of Both Worlds and would only include songs from the Roth and Hagar era. The notion of a reunion tour to coincide with the album release was floated as talks between Hagar and the Van Halen brothers progressed and became more cordial. Eddie and Alex invited Hagar to 5150 for an exploratory meeting. In his 2011 autobiography Red: My Uncensored Life in Rock, he described the events of the day in terrifying detail, alarmed everyone who read it.

He had a divorce, Hagar wrote. Valerie had vanished. The sixteen thousand square foot house that he and Valerie had constructed before she left was where he finally extended the invitation to me. There appeared to be a vampire community. Cans and bottles littered the floor in all directions. There were webs of spiders everywhere. He had a cushion and blanket and was dozing off on the floor. The cabinets didn't contain any food. Never in my life had I seen a place so filthy.

I had not seen him in ten years. He appeared to have not taken a bath in a week. He has undoubtedly not changed his clothes in at least that much time. He didn't have a shirt on. He was wearing an enormous jacket and army pants that were held up by a rope and were torn and ragged at the cuffs. Never in my life had I seen anybody so tiny. His remaining teeth were all black, and he was missing a number of teeth.

In 2019, Hagar told me, "I received a lot of backlash from ardent Eddie fans for what I said about him in my book, but I was kind to the man." 'It was gruesome, careless, and violent. I should have told my partner when I first saw his mess, "Al, you know what, let's get together some other time, come back in a year." I rarely say I'd do things differently, but in this case I should have canceled the entire tour.

"I wanted to do it for the fans and for myself," the singer said. "Getting kicked out of a band like that left me with a little grudge and an attitude for a long time." You always carry a small amount of internal hurt. It's similar to getting dumped by a girlfriend in that you always want to try again or find a new, hotter girlfriend to slam it in her face. I had some luggage, and I kind of reasoned that if we took the tour, it would get rid of the luggage, allowing me to go on. Or I could continue playing in this band indefinitely because I think it's amazing and I adore it. I was looking for resolution since I had a bad feeling about the Van Halen band I was a part of. We didn't pass away naturally. However, it was dreadful and the worst thing to ever occur. In my heart and soul, that made Eddie look so terrible.

The Best of Both Worlds, a 36-track double album with three new Hagar-fronted songs, "It's About Time," "Up for Breakfast," and "Learning to See," was scheduled for release on July 20, 2004, and the Van Halen Tour 2004 was scheduled to start on June 11 in Greensboro, North Carolina, and end on November 19 in Tucson,

Arizona, with a total of 80 shows. For reasons that were never fully explained, Eddie didn't want Michael Anthony to be a part of the tour and only approved the bassist's involvement when Anthony agreed to sign away all of his rights to the Van Halen brand and logo with the band's new management, Irving Azoff. Sammy Hagar at least thought that the tour's opening night was "phenomenal," despite all the turmoil that was going on behind the scenes. From then, things quickly took a turn for the worse. Eddie's guitar playing was so unpredictable that the band's own sound engineers frequently dropped him out of the mix due to the obvious lack of synergy between the members onstage. From the outside, it appeared as though the entire project may suddenly fail and have terrible repercussions.

Hagar claims, "It was a brutal experience." I don't say this out of rage, but there were times when I felt embarrassed to be standing next to Eddie Van Halen.When I was just browsing a website, they wrote about that trip and something to the effect of "Everything that could have gone wrong, did... and worse!" My stomach turned when I saw the image of Eddie breaking up his guitar. I was watching a clip of "It's About Time" and thought, "It's about time Eddie learned this fucking song!" I occasionally had trouble identifying the songs Eddie was playing. There is a video of us playing "Panama" while Al is screaming at Ed, who is fumbling about trying to learn the song. Come on, Ed!, Al yells as he turns to face him. "Come on, Ed!" To have to listen to such songs night after night, song after song...

There were times when we performed well, times when we were just fair to mediocre, and times when we performed horribly.I was going to leave the tour in the middle. I intended to quit after forty of the eighty shows we agreed to. After the forty-first performance, Eddie tried to break a window out of an airplane with a bottle of wine when we were flying at 40,000 feet, and I thought, "Man, I'm done." I attempted to resign, but the contract we had signed made it impossible for anyone to do so; essentially, if you left, you would have had to make up for the lost income for everyone else, which would have forced everyone into bankruptcy. Then Eddie apologized, and even though I knew the next show would be tough, I swallowed it up even though his apology meant nothing to me because he was incapable of both apologizing and actually meaning it. Michael Anthony and I would enter the arena's dressing room and wait until Eddie's guitar started playing before saying, "Well, he made it, let's go!" It wasn't enjoyable, but I always gave it my all and I never coasted through a performance.

Eddie's drinking was no longer effective for him; he was no longer able to play when intoxicated as he once could. It's a problem, and I recognized it as such. I thought, "This is fucked up, I can't be around people like this." My tolerance for alcoholics is very great because my father was such a poor alcoholic. For example, even when he was inebriated, my father would still be kind to me and I would still feel safe, so it wasn't as problematic as it may have been for my mother, for example. You can't truly impose your will on someone who can still function, but when they get so inebriated that they can't perform their duties or act in the way you expect them to, it's time to say, "Hey, hold it, you can't do that any more, and if you do, I'm outta here."

Valerie Bertinelli received a call from Alex Van Halen on December 1st asking if she would take part in yet another intervention with Eddie. That plan, however, was unsuccessful, in part because a week later, on December 8, former Pantera guitarist Darrell 'Dimebag' Abbott, a lifelong fan of Van Halen who had recently become friends with Eddie and hung out with him following the band's concert in Lubbock, Texas, on September 29, was shot and killed on stage in Columbus, Ohio, while performing with his new band, Damageplan. At the guitarist's memorial service, Eddie gave a speech at Rita Haney's suggestion. In a wonderful and moving homage, Eddie laid Dimebag's casket with the iconic yellow and black guitar he'd played on Van Halen II. But even close friends were disturbed by his unusual behavior at the memorial service.

Zakk Wylde, who had a round of shots with the guitarist during the event to honor Dimebag's legacy, said, "I don't know what the hell happened to Ed." He hasn't only lost his mind, you know. He resides in Atlantis.

David Lee Roth told Classic Rock's James McNair that "Ed's adrift right now." I believe the Van Halens are lost and have forgotten why they started out doing this. Eddie Van Halen hasn't gotten to enjoy his triumph for more than ten minutes, in my opinion.

The situation would only become stranger. The first piece of information was that Eddie was co-financing and contributing music to the pornographic film Sacred Sin, which he compared to "Braveheart with a cum shot." Then it became known that the musician had granted director Michael Ninn complete access to his home so that it could be used as a location for filming. Eddie claimed on the website of Adult Video News that he didn't care what people thought of this unconventional collaboration: "Michael Ninn is like a Spielberg to me," he added, "the imagery, the way he makes things look, just... sensual."

Eddie called into "shock jock" Howard Stern's radio show on September 8, 2006, allegedly to promote the movie. He stated that the movie would also be released in a less explicit, R-rated edition under the name Rise. The guitarist casually discounted the abilities of Jimi Hendrix and Eric Clapton (I hate to say it, but when he was a heroin addict he was good), and then asserted that he had defeated cancer "without chemo or radiation," kicking off a wide-ranging and frequently jaw-dropping 25-minute conversation. Eddie responded, "I did it in a way that is not exactly legal in this country," when Stern pressed him to explain how he'd done it. He then revealed that he and Dr. Steve McClain had formed a pathology lab, McClain Laboratories, in Smithtown, Long Island, with the goal of curing cancer.

The topic of conversation changed to Eddie's hatred of his former bandmates and Van Halen's future while his host tried to digest this startling revelation. Eddie added, "They're out there billing themselves as the Other Half of Van Halen," referring to Michael Anthony and Sammy Hagar as "Sauce Sobolewski" and "the Little Red Worm," respectively, to their tequila and hot sauce lines. The other half of Van Halen is my brother. They are out there selling tequila and hot sauce while simultaneously playing all of my music.

Wolfgang, his fifteen-year-old son, was then introduced as Van Halen's replacement bassist.

Eddie declared, "My son is in, and Sauce Sobolewski is free to do whatever the hell he wants."

Eddie said, "This kid is fucking deadly. Van Halen will soon be back in action, with Wolfgang dragging him and Alex along for the journey. Put your seatbelt on...

To Guitar World, he said, "Wolfgang breathes new life into what we're doing." He imparts youth to something that is already youthful. It's eerie, considering he's only been playing bass for three months. He twists our stuff in an amazing way while being tightly restrained. The youngster is kicking my behind!

Photographer Ross Halfin was among the first individuals outside of the band's intimate circle to hear the new-look Van Halen. On December 13, Halfin revealed that he had photographed the group in Los Angeles and had heard practice tapes that he had mistakenly believed to be dated 1978 but were actually only 48 hours old. Halfin stated that the band's performance was "jaw-droppingly amazing" and "untouchable." It was just as thrilling as when I first saw them. The addition of Edward's son on bass has given them new life. "They'll return and obliterate the world,"

Eddie gave the band's management permission to declare Van Halen back in operation on February 2, 2007.

According to the press release, "Van Halen officially announces their 2007 North American tour in what is without a doubt one of the most anticipated moments in rock and roll." 'David Lee Roth, the original frontman of Van Halen, will play 40 performances this summer alongside Eddie, Alex, and new bassist Wolfgang Van Halen for the first time since the band's 1984 debut. Fans of America's top rock band, Van Halen, can anticipate legendary, high-intensity concerts with a set list of their most famous songs.

Eddie Van Halen declares: "I am very excited to get back to the core of what made Van Halen."

For many fans, anger over the news that Michael Anthony had been fired from the band outweighed enthusiasm over Roth's comeback

Since 1982, Eddie has lamented Anthony's contributions to Van Halen, and the bassist had been subjected to humiliation after humiliation at the hands of the guitarist, including being forced to sign away his publication rights and getting paid for the disastrous 2004 tour with Sammy Hagar. Anthony was still unaware that his services were no longer needed.

He said, "I learned about that tour from the press, just like everyone else did." I kind of shrugged at that moment and said, "Whatever. Eddie will act on his desires if that is what he wants to do. What was I going to do if he wanted me out of the band and wanted Wolfgang to play bass instead?

Given the turbulence that followed the 2004 tour, there was some skepticism when the reunion dates were announced. and three weeks later, Rolling Stone deemed the recently announced tour to be "Kaput."

According to a top official at Live Nation, the massive concert organizer that ultimately capitulated in the face of the crisis surrounding guitar legend Eddie Van Halen, the Van Halen tour has been "shut down," the LA Times reported. Conversations with the business team behind the tour portray an image of a rock star who, on the spectrum of eccentric recluses in the music business, falls somewhere between Axl Rose and Michael Jackson. As a result, the Van Halen project failed before it even got off the ground.

A tour source confessed, "I cannot tell you how frustrating and absolutely nuts this has been."
In a statement posted to Van Halen's official website on March 8, Eddie confirmed the rumors and said that he was going back to treatment.

It said, "I have always felt a responsibility to give you my best, and I always will." I don't feel that I can give you my best right now. To better myself and be able to offer you the 110% I believe I owe you in the future, I have made the decision to check into a rehabilitation center. I can change some of the circumstances surrounding the 2007 Van Halen tour, but not all of them. I have the power to change, and

I can change for the best in terms of my rehab. In order to continue giving you the finest service possible, I want you to know that is precisely what I am doing. I sincerely appreciate you and hope to see you again in the future, better than before. With love, Ed

A week later, on March 12, the Guns N' Roses/Stone Temple Pilots albums of the hard rock supergroup' Velvet Revolver 'presented Van Halen with their induction into the Rock & Roll Hall of Fame. The Van Halen brothers and Roth were not present to hear Eddie praised by guitarist Slash as a "guitar genius and innovator, God to fans and musicians alike." Former members Sammy Hagar and Michael Anthony collected the honor in their absence.

Then a phoenix sprang from the flames. Eddie, Alex, Wolfgang, and David Lee Roth held a press conference on August 13 at the Four Seasons in Los Angeles to make the announcement of a 25-date arena tour that would start on September 27 in Charlotte, North Carolina, and end on December 11 in Calgary, Canada.

Roth began the press conference by saying, "This is the press conference that you probably never thought that you would see happen." "Certainly not while we are all still young, attractive, and in good shape. Everyone is invited.
Following a round of introductions for each band member, Roth turned to hug Eddie tightly before kissing the guitarist on the cheek.

Eddie began by saying, "I got a new brother," and then Roth invited any journalist with a question to ask. Michael Anthony's absence was soon brought up, but Roth dodged the question by praising the bassist as one of the band's "great alumni" and a "part of this band's history."

"And may I speak for you, Ed, as to why Wolf is in the band?" He went on. If I'm mistaken, tap me on the shoulder in the limo on the way home. However, even though we're at the top of our game—and we truly are—I can see why he wanted to play with the boy; after all, as you heard me say, he's wonderful. It is youthful, slender, and fucking savage when you hear these vocals and what the rhythm section is doing right now. "Get set."

We're a band, and we're going to continue, Eddie said in response to the question of a potential new record. A whole new beginning...

In reference to Eddie's March statement about going to rehab, Matt Linus from MTV News asked a final query as the press conference came to a conclusion. He quoted the guitarist: "You said you didn't feel like you were at your best." "Why did you decide that? Do you currently feel at your best?

Eddie answered, "None of us want to give you anything less than our best." We are performing at our peak.

Amazingly, they managed to pull it off, extending the tour until June 2008 and performing a total of 75 arena gigs. The tour, which attracted nearly a million spectators and earned $93 million, was the most successful in Van Halen's history.

Eddie was questioned about the likelihood of the foursome releasing a new album as it came to a conclusion. When the tour is complete, "we'll cross that bridge," he remarked.

After being administered the anticonvulsant Klonopin to wean him off booze and then antidepressants to wean him off Klonopin, the guitarist actually spent the remainder of the year at home nearly catatonic.

He lamented, "All I wanted to do was stop drinking." But instead, I was genuinely unable to speak. I did indeed leave. I'm not sure whatever dimension I entered, but I wasn't in this place. Coming out of this involved such a drawn-out process. It was already an accomplishment to be able to talk and communicate. You understand when you see homeless folks yet they are actually not there? I sat on the sofa for a full year. only taking in Law & Order. I was constantly recording music in the studio, but suddenly nothing.

Future days were better. In the garden of the couple's seven-acre mansion, Eddie married publicist Janie Liszewski, his girlfriend of three years, on June 27, 2009. The twenty-minute, non-denominational ceremony was administered by Alex Van Halen, an ordained minister; Wolfgang served as his father's best man; and Valerie Bertinelli was one among the invited guests. When It's Love by Van Halen was performed by a string quartet as Liszewski entered the church, and Eddie's first dance with his wife was to Joe Cocker's "You Are So Beautiful."

Eddie told Hustler magazine, "I really feel good for the first time in my life." I really don't want to discuss the sobriety trip in detail. But I'm just working on a number of things to improve my ability to stay calm and present in the moment. Looking back and saying, "Fuck, I've been doing this for more than 40 years," is an experience. Being alive is a blessing. I've never been happier or healthier.

"Janie is a gorgeous, sexy, sweet, powerful, and smart woman who loves me wholeheartedly." Naturally, the opposite is also true. I have a son who is beyond amazing and wonderful—a gift from God—and who I adore more than he can ever know. My brother Alex, who I adore utterly, makes me want to cry with happiness since I've been so fortunate to have him from the day I was born. What more could I possibly want? My life seems to be just getting started.

Inspiring his father and uncle to start jamming once more for enjoyment and the pure joy of making music for its own sake, Wolfgang planted the first seeds for the first Van Halen studio album in more than twenty years. Once this was done, the teen suggested that the two listen to some old Van Halen demos again to see if the songs still resonated with them and sparked an interest in them. The trio, along with a revitalized David Lee Roth, established the framework for the band's eleventh studio album within a few months.

Eddie said, "We went up to 5150 and started jamming." As soon as you enter the studio, you see shelves upon shelves of recordings. I selected a few songs that I was familiar with and enjoyed from a collection of haphazard tapes. We began rearranging them and creating new scripts for them. It felt incredibly great to record the first demo of "She's the Woman" in August 2009. It had a vintage Van Halen vibe despite being contemporary. Dave was working at Henson Studios, where he likes to record, so I emailed him Pro Tools files of recordings, which completely delighted him. "Let's get going!" he exclaimed. It felt like though we had never parted when we started working with Dave again.

He said, "I was amazed how new some of the songs sounded." Was I thinking, "Did I really write that way back then?" The most shocking thing is that I composed some of those songs while I was still a senior in high school or even a junior in high school. Regardless of the time, a good idea is a good idea.

'At first, I wasn't interested in trying anything new because I thought that even if we did, the people wouldn't like it. We suddenly woke up to the fact that we were also doing this for ourselves. What we do is this.

Interscope issued A Different Kind of Truth on February 7, 2012. The thirteen-track album, which was primarily made up of revamped versions of Van Halen songs from 1974 to 1977, had a fire, a focus, and an exuberant sense of energy and adventure that few could have predicted hearing from Van Halen in their fifth decade. While 'She's the Woman,' originally recorded on the 1977 Gene Simmons demo, contained new lyrics and a new mid-song breakdown, with the original portion having already been hijacked for 'Mean Street,' the album's opening and lead-off single, 'Tattoo,' was a ballsy fresh take on club favorite 'Down in Flames. While the infectious "Blood and Fire" was instantly recognizable to die-hard fans as a reworked version of the instrumental "Ripley," recorded for the soundtrack to Cameron Crowe's 1984 film The Wild Life, the rollicking "Bullethead" was originally written in Roth's basement on the same afternoon in 1977 on which Eddie wrote "Ain't Talkin' 'Bout Love." The Trouble with Never was a great old-school rocker, the chugging, feisty "You and Your Blues" had charming vocal trade-offs and a towering chorus, and the acoustic country-blues "Stay Frosty" had warm, welcome overtones of "Ice Cream Man."

The "Heard you missed us, we're back" album by Van Halen is not only the most eagerly anticipated reunion joint in the annals of reunion joints, it is - against all reasonable expectations - a real Van Halen album, as Rob Sheffield of Rolling Stone put it. The album, which debuted at number two on the Billboard chart, also reached the Top 10 in countries like Japan, Germany, Australia, and the UK, where it peaked at number six and became the group's highest-charting album ever.

In the week leading up to the album's release, the group gave a private concert at Hollywood's Henson Studios for VIPs from the media and music business. They played a thirteen-song set that featured live premieres of "Tattoo" and "The Trouble with Never." For Noisecreep, Chris Epting praised the guitarist's performance as "masterful."

Epting noted, "His recent personal struggles seem to have been dealt with." The musician played with the enthusiasm of a teenager, finding himself in the song and tearing off one fierce solo after another. He appears a little heavier but healthier. His distinctive red and white guitar produced a variety of ethereal groans, shrieks, and rumbles. It was like watching Eddie again in one of Van Halen's iconic 1980s music videos.

The North American leg of the A Different Kind of Truth tour, which kicked up on 18 February at the KFC Yum! Center in Louisville, Kentucky, and ended on 26 June at the New Orleans Arena in Louisiana, was a resounding success, selling 448,506 tickets over the course of 49 performances. Eddie Vedder of Pearl Jam was present during the quartet's concert on May 5 at the Tacoma Dome in Washington.

Vedder later admitted to Howard Stern, "I brought Van Halen I and II on an eight-track, and that's what we cranked on the way to the Tacoma Dome." I thought, "I'm going to take that in, because we might meet him, and I might even get him to sign this damn thing!" Indeed, we did, and I must admit that I was a little uneasy because, if you're Eddie Van Halen, I would absolutely respect that. If you're Eddie Van Halen, you can be whatever you want. He turned out to be the sweetest man alive.

"Hey, Ed, would it be funny if I asked you to sign this thing?" I kind of sheepishly offer. Oh my God, look at that, he exclaimed. Wolfie come here now. This is what we used to put out, he said to

Wolfgang. He clarified it. So I have this lovely note with the words "To Eddie, from Eddie" written on it.

Eddie admitted to USA Today that the group's planned thirty-date summer tour was scrapped because "we bit off more than we could chew." Nevertheless, the band hit the road again in the spring and summer of 2013 to play in Australia and Japan, where their first live album with Roth, Tokyo Dome Live in Concert, was recorded on June 21.

Eddie acknowledged to Chris Gill of Guitar World that "there are mistakes." However, given how it sounded that evening, we decided to leave it alone. When you patch flaws or broken pieces, the experience is no longer authentic.

'Since the beginning, Van Halen has been hostile,' he claimed. "The recording's rawness increases its power." We all have this untamed energy inside of us that overflows the edges. Even if it's never truly right or flawless, it adds tension. "Okay, who's going to blow it?" is the response. [laughs] You're on the edge of your seat waiting for someone to mess up, but nobody ever does. It's simply raw. It's the genuine article.

Beyond A Different Kind of Truth's economic and critical success, Van Halen, who are now in their fifth decade, started to gain some respect outside the hard-rock scene. Eddie's "Frank 2" guitar will be on display at the Smithsonian's National Museum of American History as part of its Division of Culture and the Arts, the museum announced in February 2011. Eddie was described as a "Dutch-American guitarist, keyboardist, songwriter, producer, and self-taught inventor of guitar technology and technique" by the museum. "He is best known as the lead guitarist and co-founder of the hard-rock band Van Halen and recognized for his innovative performing and recording styles in blues-based rock, tapping, intense solos, and high-frequency feedback," the museum continued.

According to Brent D. Glass, the museum's director, "The museum collects objects that are multidimensional, and this guitar reflects

93

innovation, talent, and influence." "The guitar brings the instrument collections of the museum into more recent history."

In 2015, four years later, the guitarist accepted an invitation to the museum to participate in a series of interviews titled "What It Means to Be American."

What more could one want for than to be acknowledged as having helped bring about change, right? Billboard was told by Van Halen. It is a tremendous honor to be acknowledged as having made contributions to American music, especially as an immigrant.

The guitarist looked attractive and healthy, and he demonstrated that he was an engaging, eloquent, and perceptive speaker, holding the sold-out audience rapt throughout his talk with music journalist Denise Quan. He was unrecognizably different from the emaciated, shattered person Sammy Hagar depicted in Red. When asked for the key to Van Halen's longevity, he related a Dutch proverb that translates to "just keep pedaling," which his father Jan frequently used.

Eddie said, "I'm always pushing things past where [they're] supposed to be." Spinal Tap was turning 11 when I turned 15.
Do you think you're living the American Dream, Quan questioned.

Eddie retorted, looking out at his brother and son in the audience, "We came here with about $50 and a piano, and we didn't speak the language." 'Look at where we are now. What is the American Dream if not that?

***

2018 saw the start of rumors that Van Halen was planning a massive stadium tour throughout the globe to cap off their incredible career. As a sign of respect for Van Halen's revolutionary contributions to the rock 'n' roll scene, word circulated across the music industry that superstar bands like Metallica and Foo Fighters, stadium headliners in their own right, were willing to support the band on certain dates. Sammy Hagar has a unique perspective on how things might develop. When asked if money was a factor in his decision to rejoin the group, he responded, "Oh, fuck, I would do it for free... If I had it right, four adults may be there.

I would love to do a record with Eddie, Alex, and Michael in a heartbeat, he insisted, "if we could elevate ourselves out of the cesspool that we fell into, have a nice shower, put on some fresh clothes, and go out and see who we are today." I would only want to go on tour with Eddie, Alex, Michael, and Dave, according to the singer. Dave would perform songs like "You Really Got Me" and "Runnin' with the Devil" before I would come out and Dave would perform "Why Can't This Be Love" and "Best of Both Worlds" before he would come back out again, and so on. We would refer to this performance as The Best of Both Worlds, and we would take it somewhat chronologically. It would be for the Van Halen supporters and a fitting manner to end the band's career. That's where my head is at, but I don't know where everyone else is.

Whether or not the Van Halens or their manager Irving Azoff ever gave Hagar's suggestion any thought, the group soon had other important issues to think about. When David Lee Roth said, "I think Van Halen's finished," in September 2019, it was the first indication that unanticipated circumstances were working together to block the start of a new Van Halen tour.

A question concerning rumors of a full band tour was dismissed by Roth during a radio interview to promote his upcoming solo residency in Las Vegas in 2020, responding, "I think Van Halen's finished and this is the next phase." Whatever that means, I have de facto inherited the band. Van Halen won't be making a comeback in the way that you may expect.

However, he continued, "Eddie Van Halen has his own story to tell; it's not mine to tell."

By adding to this statement, the singer told the New York Times, "I don't know that Eddie Van Halen is ever really going to rally for the rigors of the road again," to which Wolfgang replied, "I don't really think that's up to him [Roth] to decide."

This unusually direct response from Eddie's son, who is generally respectful and diplomatic, grabbed some attention. But it did not prepare anyone for the information that Wolfgang will provide on October 6, 2020.

My father, Edward Lodewijk Van Halen, ended his protracted and grueling battle with cancer this morning, and I can't believe I have to write this. He was the ideal parent a child could have. Each and every second I spent with him, both on and off stage, was a treasure. I don't think I'll ever totally get over this loss, and my heart is devastated. Pop, I adore you so much.

The rock community and beyond responded to the shocking news with an enormous outpouring of sadness. The guitarist and Sammy Hagar had lately made up, and the singer described himself as "heartbroken and speechless." Brian May of Queen stated that the news "punched a big hole in my heart."

He commented, "This wonderful man was way too young to be taken." What a gift, what a legacy—possibly the most innovative and brilliant rock guitarist in history. I picture him as a young boy, an innocent prodigy who was always joyful and modest. His truly amazing fingertips unlocked the door to a whole new world of playing. I love the times we spent together.

Slash, the guitarist for Guns N' Roses, shared a single, monochrome photo of Van Halen holding his custom-built "Frankenstrat" guitar on Instagram along with the hashtag "RIP #EddieVanHalen."

Beach Boy Brian Wilson commented, "I just learned about Eddie Van Halen and I feel terrible about it." Eddie was a fantastic guitarist, and I recall how popular Van Halen was, particularly in Los Angeles. Regards and mercy to Eddie's loved ones.

Irving Azoff remarked, "I probably can't speak as well about Ed's musical genius as others have spoken over the last 24 hours, but Ed the human being, especially as he had to come to terms with being human, really shone." He made a wonderful father. You have this impression of this brash, extraordinary, noisy prodigy, but he actually had a great heart.

Tony Iommi's remembrance of his old friend has an extra sadness because he has just battled cancer himself.

Iommi remarked, "I'm just heartbroken to hear the news of the passing of my dear friend Eddie Van Halen." He fought his cancer for a very long time and valiantly all the way to the end. Eddie was a very unique individual and a really good friend. Until we cross paths again, rest in peace, my beloved friend.

In response to the news, David Lee Roth shared a black-and-white photo taken by Robert Yager of him and the guitarist holding hands backstage before Van Halen's 2007 'comeback' tour opener at Charlotte, North Carolina's Bobcats Arena. 'What a Long Great Trip It's Been,' his caption stated.

Eddie had died in Providence St. John's Health Center in Santa Monica, California, with his family by his side, it was revealed when additional information came to light. His death certificate, issued by the Los Angeles Department of Public Health, identified multiple underlying causes, including pneumonia, the bone marrow condition myelodysplastic syndrome, as well as both lung and skin cancer. His direct cause of death was described as a cerebrovascular accident, or stroke.

He was given a stage-four lung cancer diagnosis at the end of 2017 and told, "You have six weeks," by the medical professionals. Later, Wolfgang told Howard Stern. Then he traveled to Germany. It's incredible that I have three more years with him, whatever the fuck they do over there.
Things began to deteriorate significantly in the beginning of 2019. He had a brain tumor and had been involved in a motorcycle accident. We handled it, he underwent this bizarre treatment, and he recovered well. But as time passed, the shit just kept piling up. It just wouldn't stop.

On November 16, Wolfgang shared the video for "Distance," the first single from his band Mammoth WVH, which contained old home movies of his mother and father. This was his own moving ode to his father. He said that when writing the song's lyrics, he imagined how much I would miss him and how my life would be without him.

Wolfgang said, "I never wanted "Distance" to be the first song people heard from me, but I also thought my father would be here to celebrate its release." Although the song is deeply personal, I believe that anyone may identify with the concept of suffering a significant loss. He will get this. Pop, you are missed and loved.

In his interview with Lou Brutus of HardDrive Radio about the song, Wolfgang also disclosed that he had played "Distance" to his father just before his death.

'When I presented it to Dad for the first time, he cried when he heard it, maybe out of pride or simply the music in general,' said Wolfgang. And I doubt he recognized its meaning to me; I believe he simply saw it as a song about loss.

Every obituary that was written to honor Eddie's great ability and influence on the music industry was infused with that sense of loss. The artist, who is 65 years old, was lauded by The New York Times as "the most influential guitarist of his generation."

According to Jim Farber, "Mr. Van Halen structured his solos the same way Macy's choreographed its Fourth of July fireworks shows: shooting off rockets of sound that seemed to explode in a shower of light and color." Deeper or darker feelings seemed inconsequential in comparison to his energetic, athletic, joyful, and wry outpouring of riffs, runs, and solos.

There was a great hole left behind when Jimi Hendrix passed away in 1970. According to Jas Obrecht, there was suddenly something lacking from the music. We all pondered who the next Hendrix might be in the 1970s—the one who would transform the game Eddie fit the bill.

He belonged to the transcendent individuals who, like Jimi, altered music. The most sensitive man I've ever met, Eddie Van Halen's hands looked to be firmly connected to his heart and soul. He was only a conduit for music.

Eddie was asked if he had any advice for young guitarists who might harbor aspirations to emulate his accomplishments in one of his last significant interviews.
In the end, he said, "you've got to love what you're doing." There are no regulations. You have 12 fucking notes; use them however you see fit.

***

When Wolfgang Van Halen begged his father for his own guitar, he was twelve years old. The boy awoke on Christmas Day 2003 to find a custom-striped 5150 Kramer, a backup replica of the one his father used in the music video for "Panama." The boy discovered a Christmas card inside the instrument's case that was fashioned after the cover of a Playboy magazine and featured a blonde Playmate spilling out of a haphazardly buttoned Santa suit.

Wolfgang responded, "Play, boy," to Classic Rock, still giggling at the memory of understanding his father's ironic allusion. He was very pleased with his joke.
Wolfgang said, "My dad wasn't the best teacher." He commanded, "Do this." I then said, "Fuck you!" That is not something I can accomplish! Eddie Van Halen is you! What the hell am I doing there? [Laughs]
Despite this, Wolfgang picked up the guitar, bass, drums, and keyboards quickly. Consequently, he plays every instrument and sings every note on his 2021 album Mammoth WVH, which was named in honor of his father's teen covers band. It was released on June 11, 2021, and it's a strong contender for the year's best modern rock album, drawing inspiration from Foo Fighters, Alter Bridge, Jimmy Eat World, and Muse. While the thirty-year-old musician successfully asserts his own personality on this collection, there are also subtly inherited elements, such as the guitar solo on "Mammoth," which was recorded using his father's original

"Frankenstrat," or the use of the "Sunday Afternoon in the Park" synth on the album opener "Mr. Ed."

You can sense the past, Wolfgang acknowledged. "Holding it is kind of terrifying."

In actuality, Eddie Van Halen was eager to hand the baton to his son long before he passed away.

During his 2015 "What It Means to Be American" speech, he pointed to his son and said, "Wait 'til you hear his record." My mind was blown by it.

What words of wisdom from your father did you want Wolfie to be aware of? Near the end of the interview, Quan questioned the guitarist.

Eddie puffed up his cheeks as he thought about the query.

He constantly told us that you may pick up advice on what to do and what not to do from everyone, he said.

He continued, "And if you make a mistake, try again, and smile."

People will believe you meant it if you do it that way.

Printed in Great Britain
by Amazon

31319636R00056